The Holmes Papers — Volume Two

THE ANATOMY OF HEALING PRAYER

ERNEST HOLMES

Edited and Collated by
George P. Bendall, L.H.D.

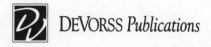
DeVorss Publications

ISBN: 0-87516-637-X
Library of Congress Card Catalogue Number:
91-71091

Second Printing, 1992

Printed in the United States of America

DeVorss & Company, Publishers
Box 550
Marina del Rey, CA 90294-0550

Contents

A Word from the Publisher

VOLUME TWO OF *The Holmes Papers, The Anatomy of Healing Prayer*, follows closely on the private publication by Dr. George Bendall of Volume One, *The Philosophy of Ernest Holmes*, making available for the first time several intimate and impromptu talks delivered by Ernest Holmes in the privacy of his close, personal circle of friends and associates in the very last year or two of his life. As such, they not only represent his most heartfelt and uninhibited feelings on a score of subjects, but they also show us the place to which Dr. Holmes' thinking had finally come after years of formulating and refining his Science of Mind philosophy as well as organizing and leading a substantial religious movement.

Most of the talks were delivered to his Tuesday Invitational Group at the Institute of Religious Science in Los Angeles. Others include his private practitioners' class. And a very special bonus here is the transcription of a recording made of Dr. Holmes' dedicatory address at the Whittier Church of Religious Science on 12 February 1959—a little more than a year before his passing—in the course of which he underwent an experience of Cosmic Consciousness that breaks dramatically into the talk, in words and in silence.

Dr. George Bendall, whose introduction as well as comments at the head of chapters provide an invaluable context, is uniquely situated to know and understand both Dr. Holmes' teaching and the man himself. Coming by irresistible attraction to the Science of Mind in the midst of a stellar career in engineering—he had been one of 200 men exempted by President Franklin D. Roosevelt from World War II military service because of their importance to the home-front industrial effort—he was later summoned by Dr. Holmes, upon the demise of Holmes' wife, to be his close associate, taking up residence at Holmes' house and serving as his personal companion during the last years of his life. Thus it was with Dr. Bendall alone that Dr. Holmes spoke about his experience of Cosmic Consciousness.

Volume One, which was initially published in a hardcover, absolutely verbatim, format—the original transcription typescript set to print, with its typos, lacunae, and Holmes' own occasional syntactical inconsistencies—is due to be reissued in a less expensive paperback format consistent with this volume, edited for clarity and coherence where necessary. Meanwhile, we launch this second volume, similarly edited but verbatim as much as possible, with no small sense of pride in furthering the exposure to the world of one of its greatest religious philosophers.

Arthur Vergara
Editor, DeVorss & Company

Introduction

THE PHILOSOPHY OF ERNEST HOLMES: THE ANATOMY OF HEALING PRAYER

D R. HOLMES WAS FOUNDER of the Church of Religious Science, and author of the book *The Science of Mind*. He was a brilliant lecturer, a keen student of logic, an avid reader, and a student of Emerson, Plato, Troward, Aurobindo, the Bible, and all other greats of the past and present.

Overlooked in his accomplishments was his extreme dedication to healing—including research into, and study of, all areas of healing. He did this by developing mental techniques and exposing principles that were immutable and that could be used. He believed in medicine, although he told me he never took a pill or medication of any kind until his late sixties. I believe he felt that from his understanding of Mary Baker Eddy's line in *Science and Health, with Key to the Scriptures*, to the effect that when all else fails, get what help is necessary and then examine your own consciousness. He expressed to me one evening, out of our many talks together, that we should prove by examination and diagnosis that a healing was taking place or had taken place.

1

He encouraged practitioners of spiritual mind healing, and some even said he favored them above other people. One incident he shared with me involved the practitioner Ivy Crane Shellhamer. She lectured in the old meditation chapel in the original Institute building. People would line up in the street to gain admission to her special hour. Many individuals claimed they had physical, mental, and emotional healings.

The other practitioners complained to Dr. Holmes that her grammar and speech were bad, and that this reflected on the Institute. They urged him to remove her from her lecture time. Ernest in his wisdom said, "When you attract as many people, and heal as many, as she does, then I'll dismiss her."

He spoke to me of studying the writings of a medical doctor in England or upstate New York, who was fifty years before his time. Several months ago the writings of a Dr. J. H. Dewey of Buffalo, New York, 1888, came into my possession. On the assumption this is whom he suggested to me, I am including from Dr. Dewey's text the following writing.

"That 'all manner of disease and all manner of sickness,' even in their apparently most hopeless forms and phases, were healed by a purely mental or spiritual influence or action, under the ministry of Christ and his Apostles, is believed by thousands. According to the record, these experiences of healing were not exceptional but were a matter of common and daily occurrence. In the majority, if not all cases, the restoration was immediate; not progressive or gradual.

"That many cases of disease in its various forms pronounced utterly hopeless by good medical authority, have been cured in our own times by a purely mental or spiritual process, thousands of reliable witnesses are ready to testify, amongst which are plenty of those thus restored. Some have been immediate and apparently miraculous, while a much larger per cent, have been gradual, some slow and others remarkably rapid, yet all absolutely healed. Some of these were healed apparently in direct answer to prayer, others at the shrine of some canonized saint, or the touch of some saintly relic, or from the water of a blessed and sacred spring, etc., and come under the head of prayer and faith cure; and others still by a direct process of what is very properly called mental treatment, under the various schools of 'Mental Healers.' Numerous failures occur under the efforts of all these various branches of modern Faith and Mental Healing. As no tabulated reports are given of the proportion of success and failure, the relative success of the different methods cannot be accurately given.

"So far as our own observation extends, these seem to be about equally divided. There are certainly remarkable successes as well as failures with them all. One fact, however, is established beyond dispute, a fact of great significance and importance. Cases absolutely beyond the reach of medical skill, and pronounced incurable by the highest medical authority, have been cured under these various methods, and in so short a period as to have all the appearance of the miraculous. These modern instances confirm the probable truth of the record of the Christ and Apostolic Healing. They certainly demonstrate the action of a law and principle, by which such perfect results are possible through a perfect understanding and application of the law and principle involved.

"That the religious opinions held by the healer or the healed have nothing whatever to do with the result, save so far as they serve to stimulate faith, is demonstrated by the fact that equally good illustrations occur under nearly every form of religious belief; and some under no religious belief at all.

"That these remarkable results are effected through the operation of some law of mental action as universal as the existence of the human mind, whether this law be understood or not, is obvious to all rational thinking. Jesus, whose success was absolute, never failing in his effort, so far as the record goes, recognized this by ascribing the marvellous cures wrought under his hands to the excercise of faith. 'Thy faith hath made thee whole,' was a common remark to the one healed. He doubtless understood this law, the secret of which is found in his doctrine of Faith.

"The majority of those healed by the 'Prayer Cure,' or 'Faith Cure,' believe it to have been the result of a miraculous interposition of divine grace, though some believe it to be the result of a powerful impression of the mind upon the vital processes under the influence of faith awakened by a religious experience. . . .

"The founder of the modern school of 'Metaphysical Healing,' Dr. P. P. Quimby, of Portland, Me., a remarkably successful practitioner, believed that he had discovered the true secret and law of all mental healing. This secret was the 'non-reality' of disease itself. He believed that he had discovered and demonstrated (by his success based on this discovery) that what men called disease was wholly a delusion of the mind; that in the nature of things there could be no disease; hence, that to discover the fact of this delusion in one's self, or to awaken another to the recognition of it, is to utterly banish disease or error from life. This is essentially the working basis of the purely 'Metaphysical' method.

"Whether disease be a delusion of the mind or a fact of actual experience, that it is often cured by a certain positive attitude of mind, induced by an acceptance of this doctrine, is itself a demonstration of the power of mind to overcome and banish the apparent disease from the body.

"Whether this doctrine be a satisfactory explanation of the law on which the results are based, each must decide for himself. One thing is certain—it is the attitude of mind and not the doctrine, that secures the result, though the doctrine, when accepted, may bring about the attitude of mind which Jesus termed Faith, and emphasized so fully. As this doctrine cannot readily be brought into universal acceptance, if a more satisfactory basis can be presented which can be very generally accepted, and by which this attitude of mind can be more widely and generally induced, will it not be wise and prudent to adopt and apply it, until at least something still more comprehensive and perfect is presented? . . .

"Without discussing the reality or non-reality of the physical world, it has, at least, the appearance of a past and present reality; and in this chapter we will accept the appearance for the fact.

"Disease we will define as a disturbed or deranged condition of vital action, to which all physical organisms, whether of plant, animal or man, are liable under abnormal conditions, and which in animals and men, often causes great suffering and distress. To remove the disturbance and restore the balance of harmony in the vital processes, is to remove the disease and restore the health of the sufferer.

"There is an inherent tendency in the principle of life in all organisms, whether of plant, animal or man, to spontaneously react against the disturbance, recover the lost balance, and in case of injury to the organs or tissues, either from disease or accident, to heal and restore the injured parts. This takes place in plants, the same precisely as in animals and man, and therefore is independent of mental action one way or the other. It is the spontaneous and automatic action of the healing function of life itself.

"In plant and animal the process of healing and recuperation is always gradual; never immediate nor instantaneous, yet may be hastened or hindered by external conditions. The influence of external conditions is the same also upon the healing processes in man. But the active influence of mental states upon the vital processes, and especially upon the healing function of life, is very great and may be made almost absolute. Fear which engenders distrust and despondency, is the one demoralizing mental state, and faith,

which gives assurance, confidence and trusting expectancy, is the one restoring and sustaining mental
state. The problem of mental influence on health and
disease is involved in these two opposing states.

"The functions of life as manifest in the processes
of growth, repair, and reproduction, are spontaneous and automatic, and exist and operate independent of thought and mental influence, the same in
man as in the plant; but where mind exists and is active, as in man, with free powers of choice and volition, it becomes the most direct and potent power
to disturb the vital processes and induce disease, or
to sustain them in their highest vigor, and so prevent
or cure disease. It is through this direct influence of
mental states over the vital processes, that immediate healing occurs so often in man, while it is always
gradual in animals and plants.

"It has been demonstrated, however, that the human mind is capable of affecting the vital processes
and the springs of life in animals and plants, by the
concentration of attention in desire and faith upon
them also to this end. . . .

"The 'Metaphysical' theory starts out with the assumption that all supposed bodily conditions,
whether of health or disease, are wholly the reflection of mental states, and therefore that the mind,
and not the body, is the only proper subject of con-
sideration and treatment.

"While the mind is capable of inducing nearly if not
quite all forms of disease, it obviously cannot produce a sliver in the flesh, or other external catastro-
phe; neither do all bodily derangements originate in

mind any more than do injuries, however, from external and physical causes, the mind is just as potent in quickening the restoration and healing action of life, as though the disease itself originated in mental disturbance.

"With these explanations we may proceed to consider the physical as well as the spiritual basis of healing through mental action and supremacy, without being misunderstood. Our object is not to discuss theories as such, pro or con, but to consider the one law operating under all these theories; for as Spirit and Life are one, there can be but one law of health and healing though many conditions may be involved.

"There is but one power of healing, and that is lodged in the life of the individual; the same in plants and animals as in man. This power may be disturbed and its normal action prevented by various influences and conditions, and by the operation of the same law it may be quickened and reinforced by the appropriate influences and conditions.

"On the recognition of this principle all medical and hygienic measures are based, whether they be wise or foolish. Mental or Faith healing is but the substitution of mental therapeutics for the external measures of the other schools, medical and hygienic.

"If, as we think, it has been fully demonstrated in experience, that the mind itself in its various states and moods, is the most potent agent known in its direct influence upon vital processes of the organism in which it is manifest, either to exalt or depress, derange or restore; then the mental therapeutists are destined sooner or later to supplant all other schools.

"Every honest experimental effort in this direction should be encouraged; not opposed and ridiculed, as is too apt to be the case, from the stand-point of time-honored traditional bigotry and error, set with a flint-like prejudice against all advancing innovations.

"It is hardly possible to introduce an error under the head of mental therapeutics, so absurd in its nature, or disastrous in its result, as many which have been taught in the name of science, and indorsed and cherished by all the most popular medical colleges of the world.

"The one strong feature of the 'Metaphysical' school is its full recognition and positive affirmation of the absolute supremacy of mind over all supposed physical laws and conditions. This is practically true, and hence a truth of supreme importance. But the mind even in this supremacy, must operate in obedience to certain established laws and conditions. Through ignorance it is itself brought into bondage even to physical conditions, and is liberated only through enlightenment. It can assert and maintain its freedom only as it understands and obeys the law of its freedom and supremacy.

"Faith is the attitude of mind which crowns it with supreme power, but there must be a rational and demonstrable basis for the excercise of this faith. Faith is not credulity nor a blind adherence to creed and dogma, nor acceptance of any arbitrary authority whatever. This is superstition. True faith is perfect confidence and trust in the unvarying operation of recognized and established laws."

GEORGE P. BENDALL

PART I

CHAPTER 1

Consciousness of Unity

I knew that someplace there was a talk given by Dr. Holmes on Unity that I had to make a part of this work. I searched and finally after Treatment a good friend, Betty Williams, gave me a copy of a talk given by Dr. Holmes to the Practitioners Group on 23rd May 1955.

Ernest always believed that the biggest danger to the practice of the teaching was the practice of dualism. The basis of all healing is the complete conviction of one undivided spiritual system—"God in and through all things."

Therefore what is known at one point is known at all points:

"I am one with God"
(Implying a separation, so that we had to glue ourselves back to God.)
"Positive and Negative Thinking"
(Implying two kinds of creative thought.)
"I have to overcome this condition"
(Implying the condition is a god.)

He constantly stressed One-One-One-One. This talk emphasizes his deep conviction.

Now we are talking about Cosmic Consciousness and what it should mean to us. As you know, we have built up a concept starting with the idea of consciousness, and starting with the concept particularly that the Infinite never expresses itself in fragments. There is no such a thing as a part of God. In an indivisible unity, all of everything is present everywhere all the time. Science has told us within the last few years that, strange as it may seem, we are on the verge of having to accustom our thinking to the concept that every physical concept which seems so confined to its particular place is present everywhere.

Now we discussed that consciousness starts by involution, and consciousness, or pure Spirit, impregnates everything. This is the principle of involution and then it is hidden in all things everywhere. But if the consciousness of God—and this is what we are talking about—or the Presence of God, or the Spirit is in everything, and if it is unbroken, and if it is undivided and does not express itself in fragments but in a totality, it is all everywhere—then all of it is incarnated in everything, as far as its potential is concerned; but in each thing it must be incarnated as the idea and the potentiality of that thing in which it is incarnated, in which it is involved, invoking in this involution everything that is going to follow in the process of evolution. It is very important that we realize that involved, incarnated, encircled within us must be the potential of everything that we shall ever evolve into. In other words, it's certain that we will never become God, the Absolute, and exhaust the potential possibility of our own evolution because if we did and we were destined to be eternal, it would be an eternal hell—if we could ever exhaust the potential possibility; but if that which is the

Cause of the potential possibility, that which is the Absolute and the final and ultimate Reality is involved in us or incarnate in us, then there isn't a *part* of it incarnated in us; *all* of it is there. The search for Divine Unity, the realization of Unity, necessitates the acceptance that there is no dividing line—that we shall expand, progress, evolve, ad infinitum, in a sequence, from where we are to any stage that we shall ever become. Out of eternal being comes everlasting becoming.

There have to be people beyond us as we are beyond tadpoles. You and I don't know what such a future evolution as we may undergo may mean. The potential of our future evolution is already inherent, latent, and, let us say, to us, asleep; or we're asleep to it. One or the other is true.

I think that theory is good enough about evolving from the lowest to the highest; but always hidden in this thing keeping evolving is the whole of it, therefore, since it is what we are, it is the potential of what we may become. Consequently, hidden within in us is everything we shall ever evolve into and everything that it is, but evolving in a sequence and in a logical and mathematical sequence ever spiraling upward. That which perpetuates itself is this self; that which extends and expresses itself is itself. It is no longer another self or a greater self descending into a lesser self. I think this is very important because we shall always go in search after it where we think it may be found, that thing which we think we do not have; and wisdom, Spiritual wisdom, starts the day that we know from now on every discovery is either a discovery of the self or related to the self in the Cosmic Mind. The self must raise the self by the self.

It is for us to realize then, that evolution is the evolving of something which is completely, entirely, and absolutely already involved. There is nothing you and I can ever know outside that within us which knows. There is nothing we can know outside the Mind principle in us which is in all things and which relates everything in harmony to itself because it is unbroken and unbreakable. Unity merely dips into that thing, and because we see it externally and detached, we create it in disharmony. That is why it is said the transcendence doesn't reconcile, it transmutes. There are sharp lines of apparent separation and apparent division in order that that which is unseparated and undivided may come to fruition and fulfillment; and believe me, that's what is back of psychological frustration. All psychological frustration is occasioned by the stoppage of a cosmic flow coming from the subterranean river of our own consciousness and flowing out into our self-expression, so that the energy tending the emotion shall find release by expansion and explosion.

Now you might say, I want to know how to use this thing and I want to be practical, and I don't want to soar only a little but a little more than a lot. Remember this, we pray through the articulation of consciousness and in no other way. We don't hypnotize people, we don't mesmerize, we don't send out thoughts to hit them in the liver or rearrange their brain cells, could they be located. That isn't what we do at all. We are not trying to reintegrate or disintegrate anything; we are trying to find that which is not disintegrated, that its substance will cast a new shadow on the pathway of this experience from the center of its own being, which is eternal harmony, eternal peace, but an eternal and dynamic need to express itself, else God Himself would long since have died of ennui.

There is such a thing as hidden splendor, and all of it is here, waiting to come alive. Eddington* tells us that intelligence *is* law acting *as* law. Now, we want to know what relationship all of this has, because all of our work is consciousness acting through our word. The word without the consciousness is like the prayer without the thought.

No treatment is complete until the thought and the thing are synchronized and are one; and when they are one, they are not two; and when they are one, the word will become flesh and dwell among us. Therefore, we study consciousness—the cosmic perception of those who have arrived at least to a state in their evolution where their vision more completely penetrated the mystery of the vision. Where they looked farther and deeper into reality than most people—and going down the pages of history as is recorded in the ancient writings and teachings in Bucke's *Cosmic Consciousness, Men Who Have Walked with God*, by Cheney, and *The Perennial Philosophy* of Huxley—you will discover what these great spiritually perceiving minds have told us about the nature of the universe in which we live.

Now if the evidence of everyone of them contradicts the evidence of every other one of them, we should have every reason to doubt the validity of their testimony; but as Evelyn Underhill† has said, "The only knowledge we

*Sir Arthur Eddington, English astronomer.
†Evelyn Underhill, English religious writer.

have of the kingdom of God or of heaven must come through the consciousness of man. The mind should swing between meditation and action." But these are the few who have known. You may be sure, since they all talked about the same thing but maybe used a different language, different terminology, they all knew of the Divine incarnation. We all have flashes of this, you know. We all see beyond the present situation and hear beyond the horizon of our present experience. Everything is built on everything else. Everything is a continuation of everything else. All of these . . . things which reproduce the energies and actions of the physical man and reproduce them without the need of using the organs of the senses to do it are merely the extensions of those organs. They are already here within us and within everybody.

Now what have these people taught us that we should know? They have taught, of course, as we have said, the unity of all life, the indivisibility of all life, therefore the omnipresence of all life. Life does not come in fragments to anybody. That is why when we treat a lawsuit we say there is no plaintiff, no defendant; we are dealing with the One Mind and One Spirit, and nothing can lie to it. In other words, it is only such degree as we carry the apparent divisibility into the citadel of unity; but you cannot carry the divisibility into that which is undivided. This is proven by the fact that Science knows no energy that will destroy itself. There may be disintegrating forces in nature but no destructive. We work only with the tools of thought backed by a consciousness of the meaning of the words we speak, which flows through the word, which is a mere mold—and molds without meaning have no substance in them, and without substance they have no action. There is a state of consciousness that can do anything, and it is not hard for it to do anything; we merely have to arrive at it by argument or meditation. In other words, we too must not try to divide the indivisible. The Pentecostal Gospel reaches very high metaphysical points in its frenzy. How do you and I know but that the fight of two tigers in the jungle reaches a very high point? Do we know that it doesn't?

There is only one of whatever it is, but in the ascension even that which appears destructive will gradually recede in order that the higher principle may take over. But this means that each interpretation of the I AM might find an echo even in our limitation, that its action must be justified by some kind of an outgoing; and for all you and I know, a cancer may be the encircling within ourselves of something that wasn't expressed in any other way and had to take some form because of its inherent urge.

The moment I begin to deny facts, I begin to feel unsafe in my own mind for fear I should discard the wrong facts. It is just because the same law that made us sick can make us well—or we won't ever be able to get well or we won't ever have been sick. Now then, we have to extend our own consciousness inward and upward if we are going to extend it outward, because it will only cast a shadow equal to its own height and breadth. This is a natural phenomenon. All of God is everything. Evolution is an eternal process; there is no ultimate evil. Therefore if we could attach our consent through identification to the idea that "the Infinite is my supply—the Lord is my shepherd, I shall not want," we would probably be better able to demonstrate what we call *things*. I believe in treating for what we have need of.

The possibility of everything is in our own consciousness, and so the great and good and wise have told us. There will come with the idea everything that is necessary to project the idea. This must be back of our consciousness of the creative agency flowing through our word. It knows how to bring means to ends because it accepts the end in the beginning, and the sequence of evolution between those is already instinctive in that which impregnates the Divine fertility with the seed of an idea. Here's the mother principle which all have recognized and which should mean a great deal to us then. They have told us that this thing is love, it is beauty, it is of course power; it is peace, it is joy, it is eternal bliss—but it is not eternal inertia; it is eternal action, but an action with such complete harmony that to us it doesn't seem like action.

Within every action there is the possibility of another kind of action more swift in its speed, revolving at the center, which would dissipate the crudeness of the external action, and this is why it is that people who have arrived at any consciousness—whether it be peace, joy, faith—influence everything around them without doing anything about it. How far that little candle sheds its light! And everything that is in the nature of evil, of disillusionment, of pain, of fear, of death—everything that is of the nature of the ignorance of the Truth of the Reality—is still the Reality showing us the only face that we have learned to look at.

Everything that is of the nature of limitation is but the Limitless flowing through us at the level of our acceptance of life. Therefore we are not fighting the evil with the good, or the less with the more, or the wrong with the right; we are merely establishing at a higher level the action of that which is eternal and perfect. They have all taught us that there is no need to fear for our own soul in the Cosmos. Browning said, "I shall arrive as birds pursue their trackless path;/ The destiny is certain, the goal is sure." The path is set, but now our individualization steps in.

We find every reason in the world why we cannot enjoy life. Don't we, all the time? It is so very difficult for us to accept our good each day. We have this morbid example of all the tragedy that the world has gone through in its evolution—creative mind, mortal mind, carnal mind, it doesn't matter what you call it. Then we have the psychic impressions that press hard against our unconscious, insinuating themselves as cosmic realities, until even the revelation from the eternal God has to be strained through the hallucination of the very temporal man, the very finite man. It doesn't penetrate that cosmic reality which some of these great minds have. If we can gradually learn to drop the morbid by reaching back into the substance of that which is beyond all shadows and abiding in it—this is the secret place of the Most High.

So if you say, What's this got to do with practice?: There is a physical healing; there is a psychological healing. There is a physical cure; there is a psychological cure. There is only one kind of healing and that's spiritual, and so the spiritual may attend the mental and physical that it may be permanent. It is inevitable some day the spiritual awareness will consciously accompany physical and mental healing. What we practice is spiritual mind healing. You cannot divorce spiritual awareness from the kind of mind healing that we practice any more than you can take heat out of fire. It is only as we blend, as best we know how, our highest mental equivalent of what we think is the greatest good that we look back deeply enough to draw that good out by identification, and every identification will bring the utility of progression. The mind of a spiritual practitioner, as it were, does swing between the meditation of the wholeness and the application of that which at that moment comes to it with the announcement of its word, which is identified by the thing that it is working for; and in this way alone can it bring heaven to earth.

CHAPTER 2

The Healing Light

In June of 1958, eight months before the memorable experience of Cosmic Consciousness at Whittier, Ernest Holmes talked to a group of students about the light. Dr. Holmes felt we all were aware of light as a result of deep meditation, if only for an instant. "Let there be light, and there was light."

His method as we shared together in our talks was to have a mental equivalent of a healthy organ, tissue, nerve, or blood cell radiating a vibrant energy of light. His logic was that, the human form being a perfect creation of God's Body, it would manifest the light of Pure, Divine Energy. We prayed to recognize that light beneath the darkness of apparent symptoms of disease or disorder.

I WOULD LIKE TO talk a little about the concept of light in the universe. In the temple over the altar a light always shone. This light of course always is a symbol of the life that is never extinguished. Ye are the candle of the Lord—ye are the light of the world —let your light so shine that men seeing your good works shall glorify your Father which is in heaven. All these references to light which we find in sacred scriptures—you will find it in many of the Catholic Saints, like St. Teresa. She said the light was so strong that it was complete darkness. In other words, she is describing a light which makes everything look dark in comparison. There was a light around Jesus. When Moses came down from the mountain—this is a symbol, you know; probably Moses didn't go up into a mountain, and it doesn't matter whether he did or didn't —but there was a light around him, and they could not look upon him; and it was the same way with Jesus.

Now this light is real. There is such a light at the center of everything and you might, someday in ordinary affairs, not realizing it, look up and see that light—you might see it everywhere in all things. There is a light at the center of everyone, but it does seem that while, by reason of any fact, this light is never obliterated, it is obscured. Jesus said you don't put your light under a bushel. There is a light in every organ of the physical body. If any organ would be restored to the vibration of that light, it would become healed, because that light is the pattern of that thing. You see, everything individualized is universalized.

For instance, I have a friend who practices this thing with a certain electrical mechanics, and it seems that whatever has a liver—a bird or animal, or man or fish— there is only one rate of vibration of the liver. This shows the universality of the pattern, doesn't it? If that rate of vibration—if anybody's liver physically were tuned into the natural vibration, even if the physical liver is in a so-called diseased condition—if this were tuned into the rate of vibration which is the rate of liver, whatever that is, it would be healed. If it were caused by some mental state, you might get a bad liver again. But this is manifestation meeting manifestation externally. But it is enough to know it tends to demonstrate the universality of all things that become, we think, individual—but in reality they only become individualized.

You see, if you have an "individual" something, you will have it separate from the rest, as we discussed a few minutes ago. You can have an individuation of anything and of all things, so that each individuation merely comes to a point of universality, like that, flowing down into this point. Therefore, all of the universality of that thing is epitomized and pressing against this particular point in its infinity, which differentiates the universality without destroying its unity. It individualizes it without destroying the universality back of this individuation. It is necessary for us to conceive this because back of what you are and back of what I am is all that there is, surging to express what you are and what I am, and for us and to us nothing else.

Well, at first this might sound like a conceited concept and we say, "Does God spend all his time thinking about me?" Yes, God spends all his time thinking about me. But since God is undivided and indivisible and infinite, God spends all of his time thinking about you. Now somehow or other, we have to tune in to this universal, which is now individualized in us, because in it is our pattern, in it is our perfection. Augustine, whether he rationalized it or reasoned it, said, "Thou hast made us, thine we are, and our hearts are restless til they find repose in thee."

The search of every man is the discovery of himself. He doesn't know it. The search of every man is something that will make him whole. Of course, by intuition, instinctively, almost blindly, he gropes—as Tennyson said: "For what was I, an infant crying in the night, an infant crying for the light, and with no language but a cry." And as he develops his theme in "In Memoriam" he finally says: "But the feeble hands and helpless groping blindly in the darkness, touched God's right hand in that darkness, and are lifted up and strengthened." You will find the same thing in Wordsworth: "Not in loneliness but in trailing clouds in glory do we come from heaven which is our home."

You will find it in "Saul," one of the great poems of Browning, where David sings to Saul, and he begins by singing to him of the objective things—the cool silver shock of a plunge into cold water. He is playing, and Saul is in a state of melancholy; he is practically unconscious. David sits there and sings, first comparing the physical things, awakening him on that plane, and by and by, as the theme devlops, David says, "O Saul, a hand like this hand shall open the gates of new life to thee, see the Christ stand." And now Browning says of Saul, "He slowly resumes his old motions and attitudes kingly, he is Saul ye remember in glory; error had bent the broad brow from the daily communion." David is singing to Saul of the divine pattern of himself; he is awakening him, not to something that is not, but to something that is. He is awakening Saul to himself. And out of the inspiration of his song came the illumination which revealed that light which lighteth every man's path.

So the light is over the altar. We are the altar. This is a symbol that the light is within ourselves. Some day you may be looking up and you will see the tree give us light, as Moses did. It was not an illusion. This is a reality. And you will see there is a light around everything, and it can, to some degree now, be photographed in the human body; but it gets kind of murky at times, because the light doesn't shine. It shines; but we have covered it up with a bushel.

The only reason, medically or in any of the therapeutic sciences—osteopathy or chiropractic (all of which I believe in; I believe in anything that will work)—is not to put something there that wasn't there, but to reveal something that was there and make the mechanics, so that what was there may flow—that is all anybody can do. In other words all that any human ingenuity can gain is to restore us to our pattern—it is a cinch we didn't make it. You and I can't lay an egg. But the chicken is in the egg. And so as in Genesis it says: This is the generation of the time when the plant was in the seed before the seed was in the ground.

How many of you have read Troward's *The Law and the Word*? It is written to show that the whole mathematics of the creative sequence starts with the word. "In the beginning was the word, and the word was with God and the word was God, and all things were made by the word, and without the word was not anything made that was made. And the word became flesh and dwelt among us, and we beheld it." "I am the light of the world."

Now, Jesus said he came to bear witness or testimony to the truth, the truth that is in you and in me. Jesus was not the great exception but the great example. He came to witness the fact that it is necessary in the universe that such a thing as truth exists. It is equally necessary that the perception of truth is no different from its manifestation mathematically; that the mathematics will take care of themselves, if the perception is right. We go through the mathematics merely to correct the instrumentality, for the perception of that vision which is beyond those mathematics, but which still uses them because it can't help it. I mean they are still a part of the universe. The light that lighteth every man's path. And this light is at the center of everything and everyone. Someday you might be looking at someone, and you might see it, and you would see them suddenly enveloped in a light. Now, they are suddenly enveloped in a light to *you*, but they are not suddenly enveloped in a light. If they were, it was merely that you looked up suddenly and saw it. It is there, it is real.

And so we must think a lot about light symbolically; everything must become light—everything must. I don't know how to put it in words; I don't know how to say it. I know how to think it; I know it is true. There isn't anything outside this light. There isn't anything in which the light does not exist. Now, although it appears not to exist, it is there just the same. If you should see a person's aura, that is psychic. It will change in color. There will be a movement in it. According to his emotional state it will vary greatly; according to his habitual emotional and mental states it will always take a set form or pattern. But if you look deeper into this, you will begin to see a light —and the pattern will clear up.

Now, our whole work is based on the concept Perfect God, Perfect Man, and Perfect Being. Our whole practice is based on the concept that God is where we are and what we are, and that there isn't anything else. Our whole concept is partially based on the theory that whatever appears to be wrong is not wrong in itself but is the wrong arrangement of what is right. There is no dualism in the universe, as I have always said. There is not God and something else; there is no such thing as good or evil in itself. There is only what is, which automatically and mechanically reports from itself or interprets itself to us the way we look at it. "As thou seest that thou beest." Now, we may change the way we look at it—it will not change; it will not lessen its potentiality to suit us. So Troward wrote that whole book to show that the word is the beginning of everything—first intelligence, word, law, fact.

Intelligence conceives by the word; the word acting as law becomes the thing. The thing is an effect; the use of the law is an effect; the word is an effect; but the intelligence is cause. Therefore it can reformulate its word, it can speak a different word. Our whole theory of practice is based on the assumption that truth known is, or will become, demonstrated by the law of its own being reacting to the word at the level of our perception when we speak that word—and that is why it is some people's treatments are better than others'. It isn't because we are more spiritual sometimes than other times. We will never be any more spiritual than we are right now. We can't be. It is merely because at some time, some periods of time, for some reason—whatever it may be—we see more clearly, we think more clearly, we understand more definitely, the thing is more real to us: then is when you can do your best work. All the preparation we take for prayer or treatment—we call it treatment—is the preparation of seeing within ourselves that which is real and no longer comparing and making it less.

I was saying to a friend of mine—I have just returned from being up in Yosemite and Lake Tahoe, and we were discussing this—I was saying, "I have 1000 dollars; you have 1000 dollars. At least we know what 1000 dollars is, and we can take it out and spend it; we don't feel we are broke. We are all right, we are safe as we measure safety. Now 1,000,000 dollars is a thousand 1000 dollars as people measure money." (This doesn't seem to have much to do with light, but it has a lot to do with enlightenment.) He said, "Yes." I said, "All right, then why don't you say, 'I will treat you for a million dollars,' and I say, 'I will treat you for a million dollars.' I don't want a million dollars; neither one of us has any need of it, nor does anybody else. It is just a theory I have." And I said, "What is wrong with us?"

We got to thinking, and this thought came to me: There was another party with us who liked to garden, and I said to her, "Suppose tomorrow morning when you go home, you get yourself a little flowerpot and you have a shovel and a lot of dirt around there, and you go out and take a shovelful of dirt and put it in your little pot—and you have a potful of dirt, with as much dirt as the shovel held in the pot." I said, "The shovel didn't know it, and the pot didn't know it, and the dirt didn't know it. Who knew it? *You* knew it. Now you have need of a little potful of dirt, because you want to put a plant in it that God may make it grow. Just suppose for the fun of it that after you had filled your little pot from your little shovel—and the pot didn't know about it, and the shovel didn't know about it, and the dirt didn't know about it—you had a potful of dirt, which is fine—that is a demonstration.

"Now suppose you take your little shovel and say, 'Just for the fun of it, I'll dig up ten more shovelfuls and throw them over in the corner': you'll have ten more shovelfuls over in the corner—and the dirt won't know it, and the shovel won't know it, and you'll be the only one who knows it." Do you see the point? We are not doing that. We say we've got a potful of dirt; we do not realize that merely is a symbol of the level of our acceptance, a symbol of the receptacle within us which contains that acceptance, a symbol of its projection in our experience. We have a little pot. There is a lot of dirt, but we only got a potful of dirt. We didn't know there were ten other pots full, because that was all the dirt there was.

Now Jesus knew this. That is how he multiplied the loaves and fishes and turned water into wine, brought the boat immediately to the shore, and raised the dead. It was a divinely natural thing for a man at his level of understanding. It wasn't any effort. Now there is a light in us that knows these things—and that is intuition. There is a voice in us that speaks this language and was never taught it. No one ever told God what to be. That is beyond our human equivalent. I believe in the law of mental equivalents only as I believe that my gas tank will hold twenty gallons of gas—in no other sense. If it were a bigger tank, it would hold more.

But you see, if there were not another language beyond the words we use, we could never step the words we use up from their present capacity. Beyond all human mental equivalents, beyond all human experience, breaking down every precedent, there is a light that you and I have to follow. Otherwise we shall merely be going round and round and round in a vicious circle, caught in a beautiful cage, trapped in a beautiful trap, living still pretty much under the law of illusion or delusion, whichever it may be. But there has to be a word—while I believe in our mental equivalents as "the now": automatic reactions through polarity in the law of cause and effect. Remember, it was the genius of Jesus and Buddha not to have broken that law, but to have transcended it—and that is what you and I have to do, otherwise we should endlessly repeat our previous experiences on the old time track where they were born monotonously over and over and over again. I've counted my seven times over and over; seven times one are seven.

And so it is necessary that you and I in our practice shall break down whether they are what Freud said: a neurotic thought pattern will repeat itself with monotonous regularity throughout life; or whether we say we are endlessly repeating the history of the world, which I think we are psychologically, therefore physiologically, therefore economically and sociologically. But you see, if there were not a transcendent pattern, if there were not a light beyond our darkness, if this thing were merely an illusion, if it were merely a fanciful imagination, like one might have if he were intoxicated—but that isn't true at all. There is such a light; there is such a transcendence in every living thing—and if there were not, the seed would not burst its encasement and send down roots and send up shoots; if there were not, the bird would not nest, the child would not play, the butterfly would not come out of its chrysalis and spread its wings for its celestial flight. Remember this: don't be afraid of letting your imagination go. So long as you know it is lucid, there is a difference. I am not talking about people who are confused. I am talking about the only absolutely, completely clear thinkers the world has ever known. Jesus was the only normal man, in what he did, who ever lived. Shakespeare's imagination was the only normal imagination, or more nearly normal than anybody else's. The deductions of Einstein were the only normal things in that category the world has ever known.

Spiritual genius is normality, but we must not mistake psychic hallucination for spiritual genius, or a hunch for an intuition, or a word we hear for divine guidance. This is where we have to be very careful. But there is a divine imagination; there is a light that lighteth every man's path. Every great creator has had it, every great composer has had it—or it's had him. Emerson said, "Sometimes the muse too strong for the bard sits astride his neck and writes through his hands." That is creative writing, as over against mechanical writing; and that is the only great writing there is. All great writing, all great poetry, great music —all great acting, all great everything—is done under the inspiration of that thing which is the only final dancer, the only writer, the only thinker and the only doer there is.

Now, next will come the question: am I then but a puppet? am I then but marionette? am I pawn on the checkerboard? Here is a valid, extremely intelligent expression; for I have said God wrote every poem that was ever written. I was invited to hear a certain singer sing the other night, and she said, "Because you are coming, I want to give the best show I have ever given." I said, "You will, but not because I am coming." And it is very interesting: Her manager and people who work with her called me up the next day and said, "That is the best show she ever gave in her life." Well, I treated her because I knew she had a very great desire to do it because I was going to be there. I said, Well what is to stop God from singing? She is going to sing; God is going to sing. Now you see, I said God sings all the songs, dances all the dances, paints all the pictures, creates all art, writes every book, plays every game. Then we will ask, "Where do we come in? Are we then but puppets?"

Now we would be if we accepted the old theology and old philosophy of life. We wouldn't have any more meaning than as if God had spit into the cosmos and let the wind blow it. That is a terrible expression, isn't it? Guess I better change it and say *if he whistled*. Sounds a little better. This is the light that the world knows nothing about. They don't believe it; but don't try to force it on them, but be aware of it. This is God singing. It isn't an imitation of God; it doesn't obliterate her individuality— it is the only thing that accentuates it, it is the only thing that permits it. That is why Emerson said imitation is suicide. There is a place in every man's life where the reins run out the full length; there is spiritual genius hid in the commonplace. If God is omnipresent, there is the entirety of the creative urge, which pushes against everything, whether we call it the Divine Urge or the libido—it is all the same thing. The libido of psychology is the Divine Urge of metaphysics; it cannot be something else. Jesus said the Father seeketh such. The wind bloweth whence it listeth and no man knoweth from whence it cometh nor whither it goeth, and so is everyone who is born of the kingdom.

There is this Universal Artist devoting His or Its whole time to what I am saying right now, as though He had nothing else to do. As Emerson said, if I could get my bloated nothingness out of the way, if I could possess nothing and have nothing but IT, without possession or obsession, I should give full reign to Its genius at the level of my present state of evolution. But there is something beyond that, and that, and that. "Ever as the spiral grew/ he left the old house for the new."

There is a light that lighteth every man's path. Now, don't be afraid to experiment with this light; don't think you are silly if you believe in it. I have seen it many times. It is real. It is not illusionary—it is a light. So we cannot say since God dances every dance and sings every song and plays every play and writes every book . . . As Emerson said, "The mind that wrote history is the mind that reads it, and interprets it, and it can be understood or interpreted only from this basis, because human history is a record of the doings of that mind on this planet." That is the way he opens up his great essay, the greatest series of intellectual essays the world has ever known.

And so, to surrender to this genius is not conceit, because you don't surrender to it while you are conceited. That is putting a blinder on it. There has to be in everyone a light—there has to be in everyone a divinity that shapes his ends, "rough hew them though he may." There has to be behind everyone an urge and a push, and in front of him a pull that is irresistible, immutable, absolute. There has to be a word or a state of consciousness that exercises its authority to the level of our present perception. There has to be, or we wouldn't be here.

I do not believe what I believe because I believe what I want to believe—because I know that all the belief in the world will not change reality, and all the unbelief will not change it either; that your opinion and my opinion haven't a thing in the world to do with it—we are only fortunate. That is why I believe that treatment is independent of the one who gives it. It is now an entity in a field of law and will perform its office for which it was created, and nothing can stop it—unless the one who gave it denies it. He is the only one who can neutralize it. This idea that other people influence us is all nonsense. Why? Because no two things exist at the same rate of vibration and in a universe of infinity, the manifestation has to be equal to the infinity of the Manifester. You and I may not comprehend but a little of that infinity, but logically and mathematically we know it goes on and on and there is never any confinement. That is why the Talmud said, "God will doubly guide the already guided." It is why Jesus said "to him that hath shall be given."

It sounds like a pretty cold fact, but it is the truth. But the light shines in the darkness and the darkness comprehendeth it not. And Jesus is one of the chief accusers. He said, "You would be followers of the dark; you would be worshipers of the dark. Light has come into the world and you fail to receive it. You live in darkness." He wasn't condemning them; he wasn't saying, "You are going to hell." His name wasn't Billy. It was Jesus the Christ, the Illumined. There is only one of whatever it is, not two. That one is what you are. You had nothing to do with it; it is none of your business; you can't help it; you can't avoid it; and there is no use putting it off. "If ye know these things," the Bible says, "happy are ye if you do them."

Let us individually, then, in the silence of our own contemplation, take time to feel that light and see it. Very frequently—I did it last night, after I got home from having a class—I sit down all alone for two hours and just listen to the silence, and it speaks, I look into the darkness and it turns light, and it is there—and there isn't any question about it. Back of you, the Infinite searches into manifestation through you, as you, what you are—it is you. We don't have to be ashamed of it. You don't have to say, "I despise my personality; I hate this body; I am a worm of the dust," and think you are surrendering to God. This is a denial of God. All we have to say is, "There is nothing in me but God."

What we surrender to is not a foreign agent, but we acquiesce consciously in a divine host, a celestial visitor, a universal individualization, and if it is true that that exists in us and it was put there not by our will but by *the* will, who are we to deny it? If it is that way and we have reached a place in evolution where acquiescence and consent alone can reunite our present experience with that which ceased to exist when all compulsory problems of evolution ceased—"Long since, fire or mist or planet, a crystal or a cell, / a saurian and jellyfish, then caves where caveman dwell, / then a sense of law and order and a face turned from the clod, / some call it evolution, others call it God." When that day arrived in prehistoric times, that the evolutionary push had done all that could be done by compulsion, it left only the automatic reactions of the physical body to keep it going to the place of self-discovery. And from then till now and forevermore, it will be only the conscious cooperation at first between what appears to be the one and the other, and gradually the other as the one, and finally the one as the only. We are not in it or of it or with it—*we are it.* If that is true, our future evolution will be only as we perceive that light in the darkness, until the darkness isn't there—only as we accept that divine individuation: that there is that within me which is already complete. This is where the soul makes its great claim on God; this is where the Spirit that went out in search of us discovered itself; this is where the prodigal returns to the Father's house; this is where we unite with that light that lighteth everything and that light in which there is no darkness.

And for those of us who believe in these things, and without any pretense of throwing ourselves around—that has nothing to do with it—I wouldn't walk across the street to impress anyone living—that means nothing—I would walk around the world to find someone who is enlightened; that is a different thing; I would crawl on my hands and knees. It is here. Everything we go in search after, we shall overlook; looking at, shall not see; or seeing somewhat, shall interpret only in the light of that which we reflect into it from the glory which is ours. Now this is not conceit; this is a humility so terrific, so great— a humility that does not obliterate but accentuates by acquiescence. For who are we to throw a lie into the face of the Almighty and deny what the Omnipotent has decreed?

Let us then believe in that life; let us seek to see it everywhere and feel it and announce it and pronounce it, because that greatness which we recognize in Jesus and Moses and Buddha and Emerson is wonderful—if they have awakened us to a higher level of perception within ourselves. But if they have, we may know that that perception now—as we look upon them no matter how great (there are no prophets but the wise; there is no God higher than truth; there is no universe we can get out of)—if they have awakened us to that, they have merely awakened us to a self-perception of something which already existed within us. That is why Emerson said, "I go to hear a great man talk, and I don't realize that I have already given him all the greatness he has." You are great and I am great—not in conceit, not in our isolation or separation, not as though we say to others, "Look at me and die," because you and I cannot announce our greatness without including the greatness of everything that lives. Something forevermore blinds our eyes to the perception of the self unless it interprets itself everywhere. This is one of the things we fail to realize: I can claim nothing for myself with validity, realize nothing in myself, unless I find it and see it in you—because I can see only with my own eyes. Here is where there is no danger; here is where there is no conceit; here is where the spirit has no arrogance.

And I think another thing, which seems very important to me, and that is to regain in our own consciousness that spontaneity we had as a child. Somone may say, "Oh, that is nonsense and silly." That is all right. Who cares if we are silly? I would just as soon be a fool, because I know all the world is fooled; I had just as soon be wrong, because all the world is wrong; I had just as soon be a sinner (I would like it to be done artistically—because I love beauty). But we may know this: This spontaneous manifestation of life everywhere that bursts forth out of nothing into full bloom is the nature and the order of the universe. The child who is in us, before we learn to be so sophisticated and fight and deny it and quarrel with everybody and be sore at everything, is not dead; he is not asleep; we have just crowded so much experience, so much negation, that not he, but we, have forgot that celestial palace from whence we came.

Each one of us should seek that beam of light—it is there—follow it to the greater light. Light is in everything; light surrounds everything; light lights our path. But if all the arbitrary and compulsory processes of evolution have long since stopped—which I believe they have, or we would not be evolving into individuations of infinity, which we are—then our acquiescence must come of God, who can no longer pronounce himself through us or pronounce himself in us and personalize himself as us. This is the surrender. It is not the surrender of our pleasure; it is not the surrender of that which is happy; it is the surrender of that which has isolated us, or that which has clouded our vision and dumbed our memory and stifled our imagination and paralyzed our action until we are immobile and inert, walking as dead men in a city of Gods.

And we must awaken ourselves—rediscover that lost paradise, that child who was not afraid of the Universe in which he lived, that child who did not deny himself or his God, that child who had not listened to the dull, monotonous tune of condemnation, until he had isolated himself in fear from the Universe in guilt and, being antisocial, became antispiritual, and finally, for his own self-protection in the world which hurts so much, must regret until nature relieves him, which it always will—because limitation and want and lack and pain belong only to the lower order of perception. There is a place on the side of the mountain we are ascending where, like the burden of the pilgrim, there is an ascent which, having gone beyond the peaks that obstructed the light around us, reaches an apex where no longer any shadows are cast. This is the light that is spoken of that lighteth every man's path; and as you believe that you live, believe you are that light. As you believe in the possibility of your own soul, believe it is God. As you believe in God, believe in yourself.

CHAPTER 3

Healing Awareness

Jesus the great teacher said, "Physician, heal thyself." He accepted the idea that thought was a movement of consciousness and would manifest in the world of people, places, and things. Ernest Holmes disagreed with the concept of prayer of supplication to a distant God. He felt it was true that "All that the father hath is thine." Therefore we had to in effect give ourselves a "treatment for incorrect thinking."

As defined by Dr. Holmes, treatment—prayer in its proper content—is the time, process, and method necessary to the changing and redirecting of our thought, clearing the thinking of negation, doubt, and fear, causing us to perceive the ever-presence of God. Ernest suggested to his followers that when they spoke or thought of prayer it should be in this understanding. This had seemed difficult for many coming from backgrounds of restrictive prayer technique. He emphasized this in a talk to the Tuesday Invitation group on November 25, 1958.

WE WANT TO become aware of our own consciousness and its absolute oneness and fusion with all that is, so there can be nothing separate from what we ourselves are or apart from it, so that we know every word we speak is the presence and power and activity of the

41

One and Only in us as us, so that we realize the transcendence of what we are doing, that the heart and mind and intellect and the will and consciousness completely accept it and that nothing within us can reject it.

We are aware of this—that our word is the presence and power and action of love, the living Spirit almighty, and of perfection and of peace and joy and wholeness, oneness—we are aware of the infinite and limitless joy of being. All the energy that there is and all the enthusiasm there is, all the intelligence there is and all the happiness, is at the point of our consciousness, and is accepted and does flow through, in and around us effortlessly.

Now it is the law of the being of each one of us that everything that he does shall prosper, that joy shall follow him, that everything he touches shall succeed, that goodness shall surround him, that love shall flow through him to everything he touches and healing and wholeness —that everything he touches is made whole. This is the law of each one of us, and we accept the law of our own being. We accept the realization of the light and life and power and presence of the truth at the center of our being. We accept the absoluteness of that truth and our own authority in it.

Now whatever the divine pattern of reality and eternal perfection and changeless wholeness, individual in each one of us—whatever it is, we accept it and permit it to appear at the surface, unclouded, complete, perfect, whole. Now this means we accept whatever the divine pattern is for each one of us. It is a cosmic pattern individualized in and through each one of us in a unique way. We accept that, and we know there is nothing that has ever happened in our experience to reject it. It doesn't get born;

it doesn't get dead; it doesn't grow old; it doesn't change; but it makes everything change all the time—the action within the action. Now we reject every belief that in any way limits the enthusiasm for life or the zest for life or the activity of life or the degrees of age or change in the reality of life, because not one of them has any truth in it. We establish in our own consciousness and our own acceptance, and project in our own experience, that which is eternally being born from the unborn.

We know, as we look back on the belief in our past, that it has no existence, and the belief in our future has no existence, and the present has complete existence extending forward and backward and around and is completely subject to the will of the present—which will is perfect. Therefore every causation set in motion in us, around us, or through us or about us is perfect causation. Every effect produced by this perfect effect, every manifestation, is perfect manifestation. Our inward consciousness knows and comprehends and hears and understands the meaning of what we say—and the wholeness of it and the peace of it and the joy of it and the perfection of it. There is one Life, which is perfect; that is our life now, and there is no other life. Right now, there is no other life —there never was any, there doesn't seem to be any, it doesn't look as though there were any, there is no one to believe there was any, and there isn't any belief in any separation.

Now that is a good treatment—to clear the track, and according to the belief of forward and backward. I was reading something from Lao-tzu the other day in which he said, "The man who knows may be learned, the learned man may never know." Isn't this wonderful! The man who knows may be learned, the man who knows what he is talking about might be a good physicist; but there might be a good physicist who didn't know. That is the perception of all the great and the good and the wise: not to decry the so superstitious and ignorant, so unenlightened, so medieval in human history and its outlook (and it is so shocked when something comes along that is different than it is; it is like the answer of the unconscious or the subjective or the inner mind of the guy when Jesus came in and it said, "Why do you come to disturb us, O Son of David?").

Whether we call it the inertia of thought patterns as psychology does, the argument of error as Mrs. Eddy* did, or the devils talking, as the Bible does—they all mean the same thing; there aren't any devils. There is no argument of error as such, other than the monotonous repetition of accepted thought patterns, and the inertia of these patterns is like a parable of Jesus: Somebody is in want, and she goes to the judge and beats on the door in the middle of the night, and he says, "Let me alone. I am in here very comfortable and my family are all asleep in bed. Go away and come tomorrow." She just beat the door down.

This is a symbolic presentation of our approach to the thing we are talking about. She would *not* take no for an answer. We take no for an answer because we haven't had enough experience of the *yes*, so that the *no* transcends the *yes*. The apostle said, "That which I do, I would not; and that which I would, I do not. Oh miserable man that I am, who shall deliver me from the body of this death?" He is talking about the inertia of thought

*Mary Baker Eddy, founder of Christian Science.

patterns. He is talking about the thing that he would say to me if I said, "I'll go raise the dead." He would say, "No you won't."

We are all screwed up about what we think is spiritual. We think unless you put on a long face and count your beads and say the Lord's Prayer. . . . And there was a time when there wasn't any Lord's Prayer and no beads to count. How did they get as far as the beads, and who wrote the Lord's Prayer? Whoever wrote the Lord's Prayer was smarter than the prayer, or he couldn't have said it. And you are greater than every saint and sage. Any person is, for himself, greater than all the saints that ever lived, because no one can live by proxy. You go there all alone—nobody can open the door but yourself, and no one can close it but yourself. You see, if someone could open it, someone could close it—and if you could say "no" to somebody else's "yes," there is something or somebody else besides you who could say "no" to your "yes." It is only because, as Kipling said, "Each in his separate star/ Shall draw the thing as he sees it/ For the God of things as they are" that we have freedom. This freedom must, of a necessity, include what we call bondage, but it must include bondage as freedom to be bound —there can be no bondage in itself.

This is what Lao-tzu meant when he said, "The man who knows may not be learned; the learned man may never know." Because all they are watching is a process. That is good—he is not criticizing the learned man at all. In our language, we would say, No matter what the intellect may have discovered or science may have demonstrated, all of which we believe in—no matter what psychology may have proven and philosophy taught or science demonstrated, there is still a mystical element which goes beyond this, and it is very evident that there is, or there would be no science and no scientist. The scientist is himself, we will say, the mystical element that goes beyond his science, or he couldn't use his science. The artist is the mystical element that paints the picture, and if he weren't, after he had painted it he would step into it. That is why I said in our statement of conviction, God enters into every creation, which I believe, and I believe in a sort of pan-psychism, but always more than the creation—always more. I happen to believe that everything from toadstools to archangels are just varying degrees of consciousness and intelligence manifesting in infinite variations, forever ascending, in a living universe which is sentient, from "the mind that sleeps in the mineral," to whatever the Absolute is that comprehends all things within Itself, because the universe is one system.

Somebody was trying to explain to me the other night —I am not very good at mechanics—and he was trying to explain electricity, and he said that the electricity is not really generated until you press the button. I still don't understand it. But they swore to me, at least for all practical purposes, that it really has to be called on before it exists. Whether it does or doesn't, I am always likening every law in nature to our metaphysical laws, merely because God is one, the Universe is one—and as Emerson said, "Nature has but a few laws, but she plays this familiar tune over and over again"; and the Hermetic teaching says, "As above, so beneath; as below so above"— what is true on one plane is true on all, or, as Swedenborg taught, the law of correspondences; and as Jesus said, "In my father's house are many mansions"—or Jacob's ladder, ascending and descending; or the laws of parallels of Emerson.

46

Now all it means is this: There isn't any science known to men but what would prove what you and I believe. If we knew how to apply it, it would never deny it. Every law in nature has a corresponding reality, working exactly like it in Mind and Spirit; it has to have, or the universe would be two systems. There cannot be a physical universe that is separated from a mental, and a mental separated from a spiritual—and the knowledge that there cannot be is the key to spiritual mind healing, consciously used. In other words, we neither materialize Spirit nor spiritualize matter; we are not using a spiritual power to make a material law work in accord with good, and we are not using a mental power to control a physical power which is out of line. These things have no existence outside our own imagination—and in saying this, we are not denying either the physical form or its mental equivalent, but really postulating the theory that the mental image in mind, and the form it takes out there, are not two different things, but one and the same—equal, identical and interchangeable—and that consciousness is superior to both because they are the action of consciousness producing a two-faced unity of temporary liquidity and temporary solidness.

That is the basis upon which spiritual mind healing may be consciously taught. Not that you are using a good power to overthrow an evil power; that is confusion. Not that you are using a big to swallow up little; that is confusion. Not that you are using heaven to cool off hell; that is confusion. Not that you are using light to overcome darkness; there is no darkness—now this is where we get stuck: *there isn't.* It is hard for us to digest the thought that we are, right now, living in a spiritual universe whose only laws are Intelligence acting as Law.

Some people would say, "What strange things you believe!" but this is exactly what Eddington said, and exactly what Jeans* said, and what modern science is beginning to accept—because you can't get away from it. Now, whether we say, In the beginning was the Word, and all things were made by the Word, and without the Word was not anything made that is made, and the Word became flesh and dwelt among us, and we beheld it—it is all the same thing. The laws of nature are Intelligence acting as Law. The laws of the human mind are Intelligence acting as Law at the level of the human mind—and there is no such thing as the human mind, but at the level of this ignorance which we call the human mind. It still is subject to law—there is no chaos in the Universe; there is no place where Law is not. If there were, there would be a place where chaos is, and if there were one place in an infinity of unity where chaos was, the whole works would blow up.

And yet we mistakenly physically try to treat any organ of the body as though it were separate from the rest of it. That is a fallacy too. You can't get a pill that will hit the liver and leave out everything else. In the Bible it says, "Awake thou that sleepest and arise from the dead, and Christ shall give thee light." Emerson said it seemed as though when we came here somebody gave us a drink too strong and we are hypnotized. And he said, once in a while we sit up and look about us but soon fall back into this stupor. It is one of the reasons why I don't believe in any of these extraordinary drugs that people are taking. I think they are good for medical experiment. I wouldn't want to arrive by any artificial effort.

*Sir James Jeans, English physicist, astronomer, and author.

In other words, only in the most intense self-awareness, independent of other things, do we arrive at that which is no longer artificial. We are caught up enough now in artificiality and pretense—not conscious, not meanly, but by the very nature of things being the way they are and the hypnosis that is imposed upon us from the cradle to the grave through negation. The very key to spiritual mind healing is a consciousness that we are living in a spiritual universe now, a living universe now, and that there is no difference between mind and what mind does, because what mind does is mind doing what mind does, no matter how solid it looks; but in that reality it is liquid.

Emerson said, "We view the universe as solid fact, God as liquid law." Now, if it is true, and I don't know, that you have to press the button before the electricity or power is called upon, and it has no existence until this connection is made, then it is also true that in a sense consciously or unconsciously a demand must be made upon the universe before it will respond. That would be true too; it would have to be true. Now, when I say a demand is made upon the universe, I don't mean waving your arms and screaming at it. The demand that is probably the most potent is the most silent; it is probably the most quiet. Lao-tzu said, "Most things are possible to him who can perfectly practice inaction." "Be still and know that I am God."

But, I guess, everything is in a response to a demand. But I think most of the demand is unconscious; most of the demand is measured out by what everyone has demanded. They said of Jesus "He breaks all of our laws, he heals people, forgives their sins, companions with sinners; he is a terrible guy." The only righteousness that they could understand was that degree of righteousness which they experienced. They were not bad people; these people weren't bad people any more than Torquemada was bad, at the Inquisition. They believed they were doing the will of God and of right to pull people's thumbnails out until they accepted the Bible instead of the sword. All these people believed they were right; "the devils also believe and tremble." Billy Graham believes he is right—probably one of the sweetest guys who ever lived, as a person; what he believes is insanity. We don't have to accept this evidence merely because a fellow is good. The insane asylum is filled with very nice people who are completely sincere.

We too are crazy from some larger viewpoint—so this isn't any criticism of the others. Probably, to someone who would know that a cancer is a thought form and know it like you and I know that ice is water—he would have this attitude toward us and say it is a thing of pain in itself. (The Chinese sage said, "O man, having the power to live, why do you die?") He would say, Dissolve it. But the human opinion is against it—the experience is against it—and we cannot deny either the experience or the human opinion. But we may affirm that which is transcendent of each and controls both because one is the other—one liquid and one apparently solid.

But there is nothing solid in the universe. Even we in our freedom do not have the freedom to destroy liberty—which is the philosophic error of Communism, and that is why it will never succeed. It is contradictory to the unity of all life individuating—completely contradictory. They may have a little concept of the unity of life in humanity; but they have lost what the unity is doing in individuating itself in differentiation without division. This is the philosophic error of Communism; it has many other errors, we think; but that is the philosophic error, and no one ever beat God at His own game, you know. "Though the mills of God grind slowly, they grind exceeding small." It is absolutely impossible for it to succeed in history.

So we are absolutists living in a world of relativity. Personally, I wish to affirm the absolutism, but I do not wish to deny the relativity for fear I will throw the baby out with the wash water—and I think too many people in our field are liable to do it. I think we have to reconcile one with the other—and will, just as soon as we know that neither the one nor the other is absolute in causation. But each would become a plaything of the gods.

Thought creates all the conditions we experience somewhere along the line, but the thinker creates his thoughts. We mess around physiologically in the physical healing and it is all right; it is good in the physical, and psychological in the mental, and they are both good. And if we can straighten them out we are going to be a lot better off. But when you and I come to give a treatment, we have to take a step up somewhere else, don't we? We have to take another step, where the reconciliation is with neither the one nor the other but with what Aurobindo calls the transcendence, which does not try to reconcile the differences, the opposites.

In other words, the heat of the sun does not try to be reconciled with the fact that an iceberg is a solid floating in a liquid and the fact that the Empire State Building could be crushed between two icebergs, because everything is the servant of what it obeys. But the heat of the sun does not try to reconcile the opposites, or the facts,

51

of big or little, right or wrong, good or evil, heaven and hell, God and the devil, hard and easy; the sun shines, and the iceberg cannot resist it, because nonresistance is the only thing that cannot be resisted. Nonviolence is the only thing that cannot be violated—it is as simple as that; but in such degree as we step down into the violence or the resistance, we are subject to the level of the violence or the resistance. Who takes up the sword will perish by it—and in such degree as he takes it up, he will be affected by it.

Now this is one of the things Lao-tzu meant when he said that the man who knows may not be learned; the man who is learned may never know. And he is right. Whether we call it that mystical element, that spiritual perception, it doesn't matter what we call it; we do deal with the transcendence in treatment, and we should know that we do. Then we do deal with that in mind which should be transcendent of our arguments through technique; and the arguments through technique are only to reach the place where we don't have to have them.

Now, I believe in using them while you need them. I believe we have a definite technique; it can be taught; it can be used, and it will work. Because we do not teach faith healing or faith manifestation, neither do we deny it. Absolute and complete faith will do it—but there are few people that have it.

Now what is the thing that happens during this process? Last Sunday evening, we went home with some friends after we dedicated the ground for Esther Barnhart's church, and I said, "Where the golden sierras keep watch over the valley's bloom" . . . and I turned around, and you couldn't see the golden sierras or the valley's blooming; but they were there just the same—but they sure didn't appear to be. We see now as through a glass darkly. But the mountain is there, and it won't move; and when they clear up the smog, that will be there which was there when there was smog. Now whatever it is that clears up the smog will not be conscious of the smog, or it will continue to get smoggier. It will be the exact opposite to it, won't it? It will be that which neutralizes it; it will be that which transcends it, no matter how it happens—it doesn't matter. The sun makes no effort to melt the iceberg—but how you and I work to get rid of something! We don't seem to get into that place of stillness.

So one of the fellows said we hadn't ought to do any of this process, and I said no, we hadn't. "Then why do you do it?" I said, "Why do *you* do it, brother? You just jump on your little horse and race down to the cemetery and raise the corpses—or shut up." In our science you have to put up or shut up. Here it is; I believe all of it. How much can we *do*? This is what is practical. Now, we must wed the practical to the ideal, because we are transcendental realists. I would never arrive at that by denying every relativity—but I could by accepting the relativity as relativity only, not subject to itself, having no law of its own isolated from the law of all being which permits it, because it expresses something that announced it. And it would seem to me if there weren't something that had to express what announced it, there would be no freedom.

In other words, I believe bondage is freedom. I believe limitation is freedom. I believe pain is freedom. (I don't like it and never had much pain—but I don't like it.) It is all right for us to believe in the relative, because we are living in relativity. We are fourth-dimensional people in a three-dimensional world. But always the fourth dimension is pressing against us, and because we don't know it, everything looks strange. I mean, it looks as though it weren't right, out here, and we try to think of that thing which will right it, and it looks as though that thing could not be. Even the truth you and I believe in seems too good to be true, doesn't it?

Even the thought of the immediacy of its availability and the absoluteness of its action seems to be too good to be true. We are running around saying, "Well, we don't know enough yet; we are not good enough yet"; and every reason we give, no matter how legitimate why it can be, makes it so that it isn't, but it is still at the *isn't* that we point. If we can understand that the *isn't* is the *is* as the *isn't*, we shall have reconciled a pair of opposites, because there are no opposites. The Gita says you have to do away with the pair of opposites before you can enter bliss, and Jesus said 'tisn't everyone who sayeth, Lord, Lord . . . and ye cannot serve both God and Mammon—this is what they are talking about, this is what Aurobindo means when he says transcendence does not reconcile, it transmutes. You could accept the iceberg as there while you watch it melt, couldn't you? Somehow or other I think we have to get rid of the resistance that we put up rightly or wrongly, but with good intentions, even in trying to get to be good. This sounds crazy, I know; but don't accept it—you don't have to take it. The studied effort to be spiritual, the unspontaneous approach to beauty will not find very much that is beautiful. "A primrose by the river's bank a yellow primrose was to him, and nothing more."

Somehow or other you and I—I guess nobody can do it for us—have to see. I gave a treatment this morning that is to work through a whole organization, in which thousands of people are engaged. There are many departments, heads of departments, stenographers, janitors—everything that goes with a big organization; and I said to myself: This statement is in every branch of this organization; there is no difference between the person who runs some department and the one who sweeps the floor—it has to affect everything and everyone for good; it has to remove every negation, every error, and everything that causes it and every belief in it, everyway; and I think I got my mental arms around the situation enough to embrace. And if I did, it will heal the whole thing just as easy as one part of it, because there are no parts in unity. Isn't that right—and I think we don't quite realize enough the sweepingness, the all-inclusiveness of what we do.

So we are fourth-dimensional people. We are spiritual beings. We are transcendent agencies living in a dimensional world, which we will always live in somewhere, and there is nothing wrong with it or it wouldn't be here. But it will not always have to obstruct us. As long as consciousness is aware, it will produce that of which it is aware. Probably we will always have a body somewhere—we are not just going to slide off into thin air, where nobody can find us. The laws of nature will persist. But we can have one that doesn't get congested and doesn't have pain and doesn't limit us and weigh anything (it doesn't have to weigh anything); it will be just as articulate.

Now we have recognized we are fourth-dimensional beings, and let's do it without being stupid and pulling a long face and looking in the mirror to see how spiritual we look and won't read anything but the Bible—and before it was written, what did they do? And when heaven and earth as we now understand it shall be rolled up like a scroll and laid away with the things that were once thought to be real—what shall we do? And so Jesus said, "Before Abraham was, I am"; "Destroy this body and that which I am will raise up another like unto it." He was both learned and he also knew. There is no reason why we may not have both, and we should have both.

We had a very successful opening in El Monte on Sunday morning, and this is a project I would like us to work on for the next month. How many of you will work on it every day? Now do it, and do it definitely, and come to a conclusion in your own mind and say, "This is the truth"—because we got off to an awfully good start in consciousness. I have a particular interest in this, not because Ed is a nice guy, but it is the first church I have started for a long time, and I want it to be—and it is—a howling success right now.

Let's stop right now, because I want to show you how I want you to treat this thing:

We are speaking the word for a new church in El Monte, and Ed Thompson is at the head of it. Now we are setting up a church in consciousness, in El Monte at the Columbia Grade School. This address is known in mind or it couldn't be named; therefore when we say this, everything that knows anything knows where it is: it is at the point of our perception, that is all; and since time comes out of the timeless and we evolute it at will, we are evoluting it for Sunday morning. Therefore when we specify Sunday morning, time and place, we create the time that will be at that place for that purpose. That is the way it works. That is the way everything works. Consequently our treatment is for that occasion and nothing else, and it has to operate on that occasion, and it will bring every person there who can be helped by being there—we don't want to waste anyone's time. It will bring everyone there who can be best served there; it will bring everyone there who can be made whole by being there. Therefore we want to get whole ourselves, so that when people come, they can be made whole. We want to let down the doorway from wholeness that heals unwholeness, so that all the power that there is will be there Sunday morning, and all the presence and all the love and healing power and all the light and all the joy and everything that is spontaneous and happy. And children will play there in the garden of God where the eternal light shines and where there is no darkness. And they will sing.

And they will dance and they will have joy and life; and even this place that is provided will not be adequate to hold them. They shall come from north and south and east and west, and this consciousness which we now have shall operate there with these other people who understand what we are doing. We are operating it. Everyone who comes in there—the healing power of that consciousness, and this consciousness, and that occasion will flow through him into perfect Light, into perfect joy, and into perfect action, into complete gladness. "I wouldn't give a nickel for a well person who isn't glad—I would rather have a corpse that is happy." At least we will get some kick out of it. This is not a droll thing; this is not a sad thing; this is not a weary thing. This is something that sings. "There is ever a song somewhere, my dear, there is ever a song." And we must sing it.

And I would have life and animation and enthusiasm that all the energy and action and power that there is in the divinity of every person coming there shall vibrate with light and life and be bound together with love and made whole, because it *is* whole. We know that the shackles shall drop from the feet of pain, and this word being the presence and the power and the activity of the living Spirit within us, it is absolute for this occasion, and we accept it in joy, and we are grateful for the privilege of speaking it—and we love it.

Now we have a pretty good consciousness right here. Let's speak it for every church in Religious Science and every practitioner. For every word that goes out on the air or anywhere else there is healing, there is wholeness, and there is joy.

Now let's turn back to the center. The only thing we shall ever really know is the center within ourselves and its relationship to all that is. This is the Life within. We make it the law of our own being, each individually: that everything he touches shall be made whole right now. Wherever he walks, there is the Light of heaven. Now let's not say "This is too good for me," or "I am not good enough for it." The Light is there anyway, and all we are doing is recognizing it—and it is there, and we are that, and we can't help it. So we may as well accept it and drop everything out of thought that denies it.

Everything we touch is quickened into action and into life and into joy and peace and into wholeness. Now let's accept the abundance—it belongs to the universe. Let's not name it as dollars and cents—it can be dollars and cents and houses and whatever you want it to be; but unless there is something there to take this form, there won't be any form. So we can know that everything that we do prospers. Now this includes everything. Maybe it is going home and making a pie. I don't know how they can make so many bad ones; it shows the creative genius of the human mind that it can take good material and make a bad product out of it. That is freedom too.

CHAPTER 4

Don't Throw the Baby Out
with the Wash Water

Ernest Holmes felt at times that too much emphasis was placed by the student of healing on techniques and study, thus sacrificing the healing feeling. Ernest had a favorite expression: "Don't get so intellectually involved that we throw the baby out with the wash water." In December of 1958, to a group of students studying to be practitioners, he expressed this idea.

Y OU ARE ALL through with the practitioner's course now, and I have nothing new to tell you. You see, we can teach techniques for practice—that is very simple —but couldn't teach someone how to be a practitioner. That would be impossible. The techniques are of the intellect, the other is of the heart, of the feeling; and I am speaking of feeling not as an emotion—not that I think there is anything wrong with emotion—but a feeling that is deeper than emotion, and a feeling in which I personally think all emotions are generated and from which all emotions flow.

We teach, as you know, two very simple but profound fundamental facts of existence: a divine Presence and a universal Law of reaction—a divine Presence which is to each one of us an Infinite Person, and which is in each one of us what we are. I was driving home from San Diego yesterday and the thought came to me about something I think would make a very good talk, which said to me (when I use that phrase I mean *I said to myself*, because there is only one self individuated in each one of us), that the overdwelling Presence is the indwelling Person. God in you as you is you. There is nothing else you can be. You didn't have anything to do with it. You didn't make it, and you can't change it. You didn't do anything that was good enough to earn it, and you can't do anything bad enough to destroy it.

I always say that at every funeral, because it is true. Life *is*; Life is self-existent. Nothing made God. The fundamental premise of our whole philosophy is that we live in a self-existent universe, self-sustaining, self-energizing, self-perpetuating, self-knowing, self-acting—and that the entire manifestation of Life exists for the delight of its Creator. We are not here to get saved—we are not lost. We are not here to glorify God—he isn't that much out of material. We are here to express That which is, and that is what accounts for all those inward feelings that everyone has, nebulous, incoherent at times, sometimes nearer the surface than at other times, but a steady persistency back of all things, an urge to live, to sing, to dance, to express life, to create.

That is why it is known that the life that doesn't create physically dies, and mentally dies, in order that it may get a new deal again, because of the congestion of the uncreated life which came with us—and we didn't do anything with it. Now whether it is a child making mud pies or a new Pope choosing his new Cardinals, one is not more important than the other in the sight of the Eternal. We are so accustomed to big and little, good and bad, up and down, over and across, right and wrong, sin and salvation, that it is difficult for us to believe this. You and I believe there is nothing but God, that there isn't anything else. God is the snail out here—this does not in any way lessen God; it *does* glorify the snail. We are each that incarnation of a divinity, and against each presses the insistent urge that will not let anyone alone because it is there: life and more life.

Now very few people understand the meaning of a spiritual universe, because they think, mistakenly, that the spiritual universe is philosophically and religiously a theory. They do not know that the universe we are looking at now is that universe—the universe we are in now. They are looking for an eternity when things will be all right. They do not know that they are in that eternity now. They are looking for a salvation which they already have, even though they are not using it with freedom and in joy. We happen to believe in a spiritual universe. Jesus said, "Behold, the kingdom of God is at hand." Probably most of them looked around and said, "We don't see anything." But he saw something and heard something and felt something that every practitioner in our field must see. The pure in heart shall see God. Now this should be interpreted literally, because where there is no longer any adulteration of Spirit and not-Spirit, of God and not-God, of Being and not-Being, there will be nothing left but what is, which is Being; and we believe in this Being.

There is a divine pattern of every cosmic manifestation, and an individual pattern of our own which I believe is the result of the sum total of the whole belief of the human race, our directly inherited tendencies, and what we have contributed to it, rightly or wrongly, wisely or unwisely. But it is necessary that we realize that we are living in a spiritual universe now, a universe which is a perfect God—that there is a perfect God, perfect man, and a perfect Being right now, and that we are experiencing it right now, and that everything that contradicts it is itself to be contradicted. Not necessarily vehemently, violently, nor by resistance; but it is to be contradicted, because it is not true. You see, if there is such a thing as a Science of Mind, there is a technique, a mental technique, applied to the recognition of something that exists before we recognize it or there would be no principle to demonstrate.

We have a principle to demonstrate; we know how to treat, technically, and in techniques; and now each one of you will have to learn from your own experience that which no one can teach you but yourself. The Gita says the self must raise the self by the self. And from Shakespeare: "To thine own self be true and it must follow as the night the day, thou canst not then be false to any man."

Every practitioner in our field has a secret with God, and that is his realization of the divine Presence to him, in him, through him, as him—because you and I will never awaken a corresponding realization in someone else beyond the level of that recognition, realization, and embodiment of the same thing. This is why Jesus said that if the blind lead the blind, they will both fall into the ditch. They say in modern psychology that in an analysis, if the one analyzing had an unredeemed psychic liability (we will say, hated his father) and the one being analyzed had an unknown psychic liability (he hated his father), when the analyst gets to the point where the patient should reveal to the analyst that he hated his father, he can't, and it is called an emotional bias which creates an intellectual blindspot. No different from Jesus saying that the blind shall lead the blind. Jesus was a great spiritual psychologist, because he knew what was in people.

So water will reach its own level by its own weight only in consciousness, in treatment, in realization, in recognition; and you will learn out of your own experience that the most intently—not intensely, but intently—you listen to the one, you can to the other. That is another way of saying Be still and know that I am God. God is all there is. At the center of everything, Whitman said, nestles the seed of perfection. The truth we have to demonstrate is that perfection *does* nestle at the center of everything. And as Browning said, it is loosing this imprisoned splendor.

Now experience has taught that we make our way by degrees through the techniques you have learned how to use, and they are correct—they are the best the world knows about; they are compiled from what is known by the world about this particular subject. Whether you call it affirmation and denial, it leads toward something which the mind no longer rejects, which the mind accepts; but now the mind *does* accept this, to all of those who have studied the metaphysical philosophies—not only ours, but many others. Ours is not better than the others; it is just the one we use. You have learned the technique and you know what its purpose is. Itself is not the creative agency; it is merely that which looses it. All the words in the world, unless they have meaning, will not do anything.

Now we have learned that the words must have a meaning to the one who gives them. You are not trying to hypnotize someone in a treatment, you don't even talk to them mentally. You are thinking in your own mind, making certain statements, perhaps, about someone. Anyone can stand in front of Lazarus and tell him to get up and come out of the tomb, but there had to be a man who wasn't afraid to roll away the stone. I don't look upon Jesus as different from other people, other than that he had something—a fullness, let us say. How he got it I don't know, and it doesn't matter, because if you throw all the bibles right out the window and all the saints and sages and saviours out of the other window, you will for the first time in your life be ready to deal with the only thing you shall ever know that will ever have an immediate perception of life.

Stop and think about that. That will be the first time you will say, "All right; God and I in space alone, and nobody else in view." That is what you have to do. There is nothing but God. Now with this has come to the metaphysical field the realization that Mind in action acts as Law. It is as simple as that: thought in action is Law. Don't say, "Why does it?" I don't know. How can a chicken lay an egg, or any of the other things happen? Nobody knows. This is life, and even God cannot explain God. You cannot explain God logically or emotionally or in any other way. That is why the ancients, some of them, said that whatever name you give It or Him, He is not that, because He is beyond that.

Now the practitioner who will the most persistently practice the Presence of God will be able to do the most with this technique. Why? Because he is filling it with a form, he is supplying it through his words with a form, he is filling the form with a feeling, like molten lava; and we could create all the intellectual forms forever and have nothing happen. Something has to fill what is called the spirit and letter of the law, I suppose, in the Bible. "My words fly upward, my thoughts remain below; words without thoughts cannot to heaven go." We believe the Universe is a spiritual system—that all the laws of the Universe are in Intelligence acting as Law. That is fundamental to our belief. There is nothing in the findings of modern science to contradict it. There is no logician who can disprove it. And the great and good and wise have always known it.

Now, Jesus understood it. He understood that in such degree as his word was consistent with the nature of reality, it was really proclaiming its nature through his word. "Not I but the Father who dwelleth in me; yet the Father is greater than I. But whatsoever things the son seeth the Father do, that also doeth the son, that the Father may be glorified in the son."

Now you embark on an experiment in practice; you are going to travel into a country no one ever went to before. All we can tell you is that there is such a country. There are a few little wheels that don't squeak so badly, but you have to do the traveling. Here you will be your only and sole teacher, not in the development of the techniques—

although you will develop techniques—but in the use of those you have; and you will discover that there is a feeling that goes with your word. Now, I am not talking about an emotion, but a deep inward indefinable something that I don't think anybody can give to anyone else. I think when we sit with, or listen to, or read books written by, people who have this thing—we get it. You know it, you recognize it, you feel it—like a song in a crowded room. That is the impartation of the language of the Invisible to Itself, or, as Plotinus* said, the flight of the Alone to the Alone, or the One to the One. It is my concept of what spiritual realization means to mental technique.

Adela Rogers [St. Johns]† had dinner with me the other night, and she was speaking about "spirituality," and I said, "Wait a minute, Adela—I don't know what you mean." She was all worked up over it—"getting spiritual" —and I told her I don't know whether I am spiritual or not. I feel like I am very close to the earth; I love the things of the earth; but I can get along without them. "Well," she said, "spirituality is that which is not materialistic or material." And I said, "There isn't any matter, Adela; matter has been dissolved in the minds of thinkers for ages, and it hasn't even a peg to hang its hat on in modern physics. There is no material universe. Therefore we don't have to contend with one! Where is a spiritual universe? Where you are looking—period." That is the end of the sentence and all of the lesson. Isn't it interesting!

Don't try to be good—you don't know what good is, and I certainly don't. They didn't think Jesus was very

*Egyptian-born Roman philosopher (A.D. 205–270).
†American journalist and popular social historian.

good. Just be yourself. Whatever is destructive is all the evil there is, and whatever is constructive is the only good there is. This is the only measuring yard, I think, and if anything does any harm, it isn't good. We believe the universe *is* a spiritual system—not as *evolving* into one—and we believe it is *now*. And, as Emerson said, we see the universe as solid fact, but God sees it as liquid law. For, he said—and this is quite a thing to have been said over a hundred years ago—matter is spirit reduced to its greatest thinness, oh so thin; and now we find it is reduced to some kind of energy and a flow, and they don't know whether it is steady or intermittent—and we don't care.

The universe in which we live is a spiritual system now —everything that is in it is a manifestation of that spiritual system now. The idea back of everything is first conceived in a generic pattern and then gradually individuated where the individual steps in and takes over at the dawn of history on this planet, I suppose. That is why the poet said, "A fire, a mist a planet; crystal and a cell./ Saurian and jellyfish; then caves where cavemen dwell./ Then a sense of law and order, and a face turned from the clod./ Some call it evolution; others call it God." We believe in evolution, but we believe evolution is the unfoldment of that which was first *in*voluted. "In the beginning was the word," etc. That at the center of everything is that which is perfect, that which is God.

Now we know that a series of affirmations and denials will produce a result—that is a technique. We know that gradually the denials turn themselves into affirmations. That is better—that is recognition. We know that as the affirmations turn themselves into that indestructible state of consciousness which can no longer be analyzed, we have what we call a realization. I think a very wonderful example, if it is true—and I don't care whether it is true or not; it is good—is Jesus standing before the tomb of Lazarus. "Father, I thank thee that thou hearest me"—this is recognition. "There is Something, and I am in cooperation with It—my Partner. This is the secret that I have with God, and I know that Thou doest always hear me." No stuttering, no stammering. Here is a man who had learned that the Universe responds to him, and he knew it. It embodies everything that is both faith and understanding, in one category. Then he says, "Lazarus, come on out!" And then they had a party.

Did you ever stop to think of that? I like parties. Now, Jesus was found at parties more than anywhere else. He wasn't a doleful . . . I was going to say, Christian, but there weren't any Christians in his time; they had never been heard of—this terrible thing had not happened to the human mind. Emerson said for every "Stoic" there *is* a Stoic, but in Christendom where is the Christian? Where is a man who would give his last shirt away? I haven't found him.

Now, we have to embody everything, and every treatment you give will be an experiment with a Principle that is absolute, with a Law that has no choice other than to respond. It is done unto you *as* you believe—good, bad, or indifferent: AS. Something bigger than you does it. It is done unto you—you do not assume the obligations of the universe. "Paul planted, Apollos watered, but God gave the increase." Emerson said it as a philosopher would say it: We are beneficiaries of the divine fact. Browning said it as a poet would say it: " 'Tis Thou, God, who giveth; 'tis I who receive." Lowell said it as a poet says it: "Bubbles we earn with a whole soul's tasking, 'tis heaven alone that is given away, 'tis only God may be had for the asking." And the sooner we stop trying to work out of our sinful lives and get over our self-condemnation, the sooner we shall no longer condemn others. Only the pure in heart shall see God, and only the meek shall inherit the earth.

There isn't the slightest chance of that ever failing. Only non-resistance shall be unresisted; only nonviolence shall never be violated. This is the law of elasticity, the fluidity of the universe in which we live, where nothing clashes but the mind of men. It is where the Bible says, "Know that in the beginning God made man perfect, but man has sought out many inventions." These are the thoughts, the feelings, the tools with which you are to deal. Real spiritual mind treatment—very little understood even by those who practice it—is not exercised while we condition anything to time, to experience, to past, to present, or to the future. Spiritual mind treatment is the spontaneous proclamation of a joyful and "a jubilant and a beholding soul," in the only time he can ever know, which is in the moment he proclaims it. No two treatments can ever be alike—there is no formula for treatment. We teach things to do, but we couldn't teach anyone living how best to do them. Could you? Who could teach a nightingale to sing? Who, having captured a nightingale and cut his throat, will have captured his song? There is always that thing which is added to our intellectual attainments—and I am not decrying the intellect; God knows that common sense is the most uncommon thing in the world. But there is that which is beyond the intellect, there is that which uses the intellect, and I personally believe in practices of what I call stretching the intellect—through identification of the individual with everything in the universe . . . the running brook . . . just as Whitman did. He was one of the greatest mystics, he was one with the water, with the foam, with the prostitute and libertine. He said, "I will reject you when the rain no longer falls on you"; and Jesus said, "Where are these thine accusers?"

Now in the mind of the practitioner in our field there must come some kind of a clearance. He can only give what he has. He can only do at the level of what he has realized; and he will have to learn to speak in an affirmative language. It isn't easy. We are not always surrounded by sweet thoughts or sweet people. There is much, not to overcome, but, let us say, to overlook. I always like something Browning said: "Oh! Thou dost all things devise and fashion for the best; / help us to see with mortal eyes, to overlook the rest." A practitioner must not be depressed by depression or elated by elation. He must not be confused by confusion. It is only as we stand above and beyond them that our word has any power over them. We do not meet resistance on the level of resistance —if we do we stay on that level. We practice a transcendence which does not deal, as the Gita says, with opposites—or as Aurobindo suggested, when he said that the transcendence does not reconcile, it transmutes. "And looking up, he said, 'Father, I thank thee' "—not looking down.

Many of the prophets of Israel and the Old Testament could never get away from seeing the valley of dry bones and the persecution of the Jews—and they still have it. It is created in their mass mind, and it will stay there till they quit it. This is nothing against them; this is cause and effect. Who is there who sees and speaks an affirmative language, who thinks affirmatively? Now, a practitioner is one whose intellect has been satisfied with the logic of his belief, because a house divided against itself cannot stand. All his intellect has been transcended by a feeling which didn't have to resort to logic.

Personally, I believe one need not contradict the other. Plotinus, whom Inge classed as the king of intellectual mystics of the ages, taught grammar and administered the estate of a number of his friends. He was a smart businessman. There is no reason why we should have a faraway look—it is the pure in heart that see God, not by some fantastic fantasy of imagination which wafts one on to a psychic sea of confusion where he thinks he is talking to Jesus and the rest of the saints and begins to go barefooted and lets his hair grow—that is all right; nothing wrong about it; sincere—and almost everybody in the insane asylum is sincere too. Jesus was right here, his feet were on the ground, his head was in the clouds, he united heaven and earth only because he said, "Behold the kingdom of God is at hand." Jesus would never have united heaven and earth through theology. He would laugh at it—well, maybe not; but he had a great sense of wit when he said, "Let him who is without sin among you cast the first stone."

He didn't call them what you and I would; and when Jesus said, "Behold," he wasn't talking about some far-off divine event toward with the whole creation moves. He was talking about what he was looking at. He was talking about what he was seeing. He was describing what he was hearing. It wasn't just a word picture, literal—

"Blessed are the pure in heart; blessed are the meek, for they shall inherit the earth." Now, Jesus inherited his earth. He wasn't a weakling. He wasn't a man beat about. Don't tell me that a man who could turn water into wine needed a winery, or to raise grapes. He didn't need a bakery; he could feed the multitude. What did he want of a bakery? He didn't need transportation; he got in the boat and immediately they were at the shore, to the annihilation of time and space as we know it—but it is true. Jesus did not need a bank account; he found money in the fish's mouth. He didn't even at the end of the trail need an undertaker, because he left nothing behind to witness to the belief that anybody is dead. Isn't this terrific!

I do not have any undue superstition about Jesus, but here is something at least we should take as a pattern and identify ourselves, I don't think with the man, but with the message. This is it: "Look unto me and be ye saved."

Now this is the spiritual element in what would otherwise be just a mental practice; and just mental practice is no good. It is that thing you can't describe. You all know what I am talking about, and yet I haven't described it. I can't and you can't, but we know there is a language which is not madness, but it is beyond the intellect. There is a testimony that comes down to us through the ages, like art and religion—the only two institutions that the ravages of time have not devastated, and they are both intuitions of the invisible. They are the language of the soul, whether it is singing or dancing or writing, painting, sculpting, or praying. Every man's life is a prayer to the God he believes in, and the God he believes in answers every man at the level of his belief. But since we are mostly hypnotized from the cradle to the grave, our level largely unconsciously is a monotonous repetition of the thoughts of the ages. I happen to believe that just as Freud said a neurotic thought pattern will repeat itself monotonously through life, so the great patterns of human belief repeat themselves generation after generation. Once in awhile someone like Emerson or Jesus breaks down the idol of the past, sees what all are looking at but very seldom see; "primrose by the river's bank a yellow primrose was to him, and nothing more."

But Jakob Böhme* looked into a geranium and saw the Kingdom of God. You and I, that is our business. Just as they have split the physical atom and disclosed solar energy, so you and I in a certain symbolic sense must split the human mental atom, until we disclose here the radiant Son of Heaven. Don't ask anybody ever if this Son exists; don't ask anybody ever if this thing is too good to be true. Don't argue with anybody about it. This is the secret you have with God, and in the silence of your own soul something answers. It doesn't answer as a word, you know; God doesn't have vocal cords like that—it doesn't come as a man with whiskers and reveal something to you that wasn't ever revealed.

There is an ear that listens to everything we think and vibrates back to us the likeness of what we thought; but because it is attuned to the infinite harmony, the range of its listening is limitless. To Jesus, it was just as natural to raise the dead as it is for us to lie down if we feel a little tired. Turning the water into wine was just a gesture of his hand. He knew of the absoluteness of the Law of Mind in action; he knew that the whole vast universe is a meditation of God, and that all the galaxies and all the

*German mystic (1575–1624).

laws and everything that govern it are individuated from the Mind that sleeps in a grain of sand, to wake to some kind of simple consciousness perhaps in a rose, a little more in an animal, and a little more in man, and on and on and on to beings as much beyond us as we are, or perhaps as Jesus himself was, beyond a tadpole—and the whole thing is a living system. And since it is Intelligence that responds to intelligence, and since its response must of a necessity be by correspondence, the Law of the Universe is to us what we are to it. The God of the Universe is more than we appear to be to It; therefore "Ever as the spiral grew, he left the old house for the new."

And don't be afraid to let something in you die, because there shall be no resurrection without a death. I am not speaking about morbidity or ceasing to be, but about hate, fear, uncertainty, just plain cussedness—everything that denies the Omnipresent Fact, the Omnipotent Power, and the beauty and the wonder of the universe in which we live, and everything that denies the overdwelling and indwelling *one* God—not two.

Now this is what practice is—it is applying mental techniques to the realization of spiritual correspondences, not visualized but felt, and tying spiritual realization through mental techniques to the Law of Mind in action, through the theory that disease, discord—everything that we deal with—is Mind in action, creating the form that causes forms objectively, to its own subjective embodiment, individually and collectively. And, as I say, we are perhaps pretty much hypnotized from the cradle to the grave, by that mass concept.

Now you engage in the practice of spiritual mind healing. I don't care whether you call it Religious Science— it doesn't matter, you know; a rose by any other name

will smell as sweet, and every moment is a fresh beginning and yesterday never happened and tomorrow hasn't
come. God and the universe have no history. That is why
Inge said, "Eternity cannot be described by straight lines,
because it is not snipped off at either end." In this moment
in which you give a treatment, right now, make it complete, make it perfect, even if you have to give another
one tomorrow. At any moment you may burst through
that shell of fear and doubt and superstition and ignorance—the dearth of spiritual realization—and find disclosed the Son of God.

Let us identify ourselves with that Sonship, with that
Presence, and with that Power, for all the power there is
and all the presence there is and all the life there is is Love,
the Living Spirit Almighty, and all the good there is is
right here in this room. The only heaven we shall ever
know is now. Behold, the kingdom of God is here. Looking long and steadfastly at the rose, we see His beauty; in
the turbulence of the wind and wave, we feel His strength;
in the softness of the raindrop on our face, we feel the
caress of the Infinite; and in the silence of the desert, a
voice speaks: "This is my beloved child." We are that.

CHAPTER 5

Change the Track of Time

A great friend of Ernest Holmes was the journalist Cobina Wright, who wrote of "Society Doings and People." This great lady was enthralled with Ernest's beliefs, and in September 1958 she interviewed him on prayer and reported his answer in a column with her byline appearing in the *Los Angeles Herald & Express* (later known as the *Herald Examiner*). The article was dated September 25, 1958, and was entitled "How to Pray Told by Church Founder." Dr. Holmes' words follow:

We all believe in prayer, and naturally we hope our prayers will be answered. Let us ask a few simple questions: What is prayer; to what do we pray; where do we pray and how do we pray?

It is self-evident, that no matter how sublime, prayer is an act of the mind based on the belief of a Power greater than itself which responds to it. Prayer is the approach we make to this Power through our thinking and believing.

Where do we pray?

Jesus gave us the answer when He said the Kingdom of God is at hand; we already live in it. Jesus had prayed in the temple since He was a child. He had also prayed by the wayside.

He found God everywhere. God is right where we are; God is always there, closer than our very breath.

But the real "where" we pray must be within ourselves. We cannot jump away from ourselves any more than we can jump away from our shadows. Our prayers are within our minds, therefore there is no place to go, as though we might find God more in one spot than another.

Sometimes we feel more peaceful and quiet in one place than another, but that does not mean there is any more of God in the desert, or on the mountain top, in a church or temple. And when we come to realize that God is already where we are, then we can realize we could just as well pray to the indwelling God on a busy street corner as anywhere else.

How should we pray?

Jesus gave us two answers to this also, when he said, when you pray believe you HAVE and you WILL receive; and another time He said that sometimes we ask and receive not, because we do not ask rightly. Let's think this through this way: God is life; therefore if we pray for life we shall receive it, but if we pray for anything that contradicts life, we couldn't hope to change the nature of God because of our petition. In other words, we pray rightly when we go along with the nature of God, and since God is love, peace, givingness, unity—we could not hope to get results through prayer if we pray contrary to these Divine attributes.

When we pray we should believe we already have what we are asking for. This is difficult, for often we are praying for things we do not now possess. We pray for happiness when we are unhappy; for abundance when we seem destitute; for peace when we are confused; companionship when we are lonely; for health when we are full of pain and suffering. It is not easy to pray for health when we are in pain, but it is possible.

We are told to pray without ceasing, for in due time we shall reap if we faint not. Anyone who practices this over a length of time will discover his whole inward thinking passing from negation to affirmation. What if it does take time and effort? Everything worth while takes time and effort.

So having complied with these few simple demands that Life makes upon us, we may pray for anything, for ourselves or others, any purpose or cause that is good. And we should EXPECT an answer. We should live in a continual expectancy of abundance, of health, of harmony, of love and friendship— merely because we believe the Kingdom of God really is at hand, and in this Kingdom is contained everything necessary to our well-being.

December 23, 1958, three months following this interview, Dr. Holmes received verbal recognition of his article while the people were assembling for the Tuesday Invitational Group meeting. Dr. Holmes then gave the following talk.

NOW LET US TURN to that divine center within us which is both God and man and know that we treat ourselves and we treat God simultaneously—we are in and of the same Presence and the same Power and the same Life. And we are the same Life because there is but One Life, that Life is God's, that Life is perfect, and that Life is our Life now—not bye and bye; right now, here and now. Now we are recognizing the supreme Spirit as the immediate spirit within us, we are recognizing God as the man which we are, in God, which is the only man there is—there is no other man. We are recognizing ourselves as the perfect, complete, whole, happy, divine, radiant consciousness of the living Spirit manifesting as the self. There is One Self, and One Life.

Emerson said it is easy enough in solitude to be independent, but he said the great man is he who in the midst of a crowd can keep with perfect simplicity the independence of his solitude. And that is so true.

Everything in manifestation runs on a time track which is a sequence of a particular chain of cause and effect. You and I do not destroy the law of cause and effect, but we can erase any sequence in it. It wouldn't be any different than going out in the garden and pulling up a certain plant you don't want there. That is running on a sequence of cause and effect, or its own time track, and all of this is but a parallel of the action and reaction that takes place in Mind and Spirit, because the Universe is only one system; and you will notice most of Jesus' illustrations in the Bible were likening the Kingdom of Heaven to what we know about nature, because Jesus knew that, as Emerson said, nature has but a few laws, but she plays them over and over.

All you have to do is squeeze the time track together, because the Alpha and Omega are but two ends of a circuit, and while it is true that in evolution it takes a long time for things to happen, remember this, Jesus did not raise the grapes or press them or distill the wine. He snapped his finger and said, "Turn the water into the other jar." He did something maybe science will do some day.

[George] Lamsa* was telling the ministers the other day about how they got the idea of the Virgin Birth, the Immaculate Conception—that in that time a woman was either a virgin or a widow, and it was always published

*Biblical scholar.

when they got married whether they were a virgin or a widow, and Mary was a virgin and Joseph was espoused to Mary. That was all there was to it, and look what they have done to the story.

Now in our imagination eliminate the process, and psychically Jesus projected his physical being from one place to another. I believe he did it; there is no reason why he shouldn't have—and all evolution then is for the purpose of uncovering and making active that which was already involuted before it became evoluted. That is why the Bible says, "I am Alpha and Omega, the beginning and end," and in Genesis it says, ". . . the generation of the time when the plant was in the seed before the seed was in the ground."

Nothing could evolve that wasn't first involved, therefore the whole process of evolution in which we believe is itself subject to that which involuted evolution. "In the beginning was the Word, and Word was with God, and the Word was God. And all things were made by the Word, and without the Word was not anything made," etc. The unique thing about our practice, and it is the only field in the world in which such practice takes place, is that we start prior to involution. Every thing out here is subject to evolution, but how many people stop to think that evolution is an effect. And involution, which precedes evolution, is also an effect. Whatever involutes is spontaneous, and whatever evolutes is mechanical. "In the beginning was the Word."

Now we start prior to involution, in treatment; we start with that which is transcendent of involution, consequently it automatically controls evolution. It is very important for us to understand this, because if we subject our treatment, our prayer, our belief to what is already involuted or spoken, it will be subject to the time track that now exists of any sequence. But if we start in this process, we are servants of the thing we obey; consequently, Troward said, we must turn resolutely from anything that suggests that what we are seeking to do is subject to either the past, the present, or the future—because the sequence of the creative cause starts with pure Intelligence and nothing else; then Intelligence in motion, which involutes; then involution in motion, which evolutes—and the only thing that is spontaneous, the only thing that has self-awareness, is the act of involution, setting the chain in motion.

Troward said we start with pure absolute Intelligence. The movement of Intelligence upon itself, which sets in motion the law of its own being, produces the manifestation of the Word. But the Word is the only thing that knows itself—all other processes are mechanical—and we start, then, with that from two motivations: to set in motion a new sequence of cause and effect, something that never happened before; or perhaps to erase an old one. It has been discovered that denial will tend to erase it, and affirmation will most certainly create a new one. But in such degree as we subject our word, our treatment, to anything that is in a process, we are making the process comply with that word and consciously or unconsciously, ignorantly or not, we are subjecting the possibility of the manifestation of this thing to the limitation of the sequence already set in motion. Therefore we have to turn away from it—and this is the difficult thing and why Jesus said, "Judge not according to appearances." Now we do it. Every scientist does it.

A friend asked if I ever talked with atheists or agnostics, and I said, there isn't any such thing. The thing that makes a person think he is one isn't that he doesn't believe in something; it is that he doesn't believe in the way people believe in something. In other words, their revolt is against theology and dogma and superstition and ignorance, and I don't blame them. And he asked what would be the main objection to believing as we believe, and I was interested he said "we," which is the first time he ever said this—and I just let it alone and said nothing. I never try to "sell" what we believe, because if we try to sell it, they won't buy it anyway, and it is only when we "do" it that someone will want to buy it. I said the materialists believe in intelligence in the universe but not in consciousness, and he asked what is the difference. I said a thing can be intelligent without being aware. The universe is governed intelligently. The materialists see the intelligence at work but they will not believe that there is a consciousness in the intelligence—a self-awareness. But it is a very peculiar thing to me, because they themselves maintain the prerogative of accepting or rejecting, and all that self-awareness is, is awareness operating at the level of self-knowingness rather than compulsion.

The Universe is governed by intelligence, but we believe that on top of intelligence there is consciousness, self-awareness—there is a perceiver as well as the act of perception, and the law set in motion by the perception. And of course this is right, because even to deny it would affirm the prerogative of not accepting it, and the moment one affirms a prerogative of conscious rejection, he has passed from the field of mechanical reaction into a field of spontaneous choice, else he couldn't do the one and not the other.

The very fact that you and I are talking is proof enough

that the Universe, as I said the other day to him, contains an Infinite Awareness which we do not understand other than at the level of our own awareness, because our own awareness is It at that level—and we will never find any other God. But we will find plenty more of this One Cause. We are never going to use it up, just because we aren't going to find it someplace else—and that is the essence of the great spiritual philosophies of the ages, is the very epitome of everything we believe. It is the thing Jesus understood, perhaps better than any other single individual; but as Lamsa was telling us the other day, Jesus did nothing new. He put in a more simple language that which he had learned from childhood, which I don't doubt, but he added to it a personal element—the complement to the Mosaic law of impersonality—and made the Universe a living thing in the consciousness of every person, in the only place that he can experience anything: he experiences all things at the level of his comprehension of that which he experiences.

But it goes further than that—he partakes of the creative process of the original cause. Jesus said, "As the Father hath life within Himself, so hath he given it to the Son to have life within himself, that whatsoever things the Son seeth the Father do, that doeth the Son also, that the Father may be glorified in the Son." In other words, what Jesus was saying was, just as God, or the First cause, is Absolute Life, so your life is the same Absolute Life (so hath He given it to the Son within Himself), and it is the same Life; it isn't apart from It, it isn't approaching It—it is It.

And again we have to realize the Ancient of Days, the Changeless, the Truth to which nothing has ever happened—because God has no history, as such. If God had a history, there is nothing you and I could do but lie right down and say, Let it happen anytime now. Therefore as Emerson said, the Ancient of Days is in the latest invention—wherever we think, the Originating Creative Intelligence that sets the Universe in place is thinking, knowing with the awareness, the same Intelligence, backed by the same Law, as it was when it spoke the nebulae into existence—because they are being spoken into existence everywhere.

Creation is going on. The Universe is a spiritual system, can't run down and can't wear out, and now that Thing is what we are at the level of our intelligence, our awareness, our consciousness. We cannot change It; we can change our own level only by stretching out our own awareness, our own consciousness, our own intellect. But we come up against new fields that sometimes baffle us because we try to get our arms around the ways and the means, not knowing that they flow out of the Cause. This is why we say we choose but we don't outline. We can't help but choose, because if we chose not to choose, we would be choosing just as much as though we chose to choose. There is no difference.

It is like people in our field who say, "Well, I don't believe in treating for money, I don't believe in being material," and I ask what they *do* treat for, and they say, "I treat to know that God's idea has everything it needs." And so I say, "What do you think you are thinking about if you want money subjectively? Why would money come instead of food?" People, including lots of us, are stupid, superstitious, and ignorant, and they can't impersonalize a Law to the extent that it knows nothing about good and bad; big and little; yesterday, today, and to-morrow; and has no history, but in the split second of our perception spontaneously flows into something that even it never did before. Because if God didn't do something right this minute in me—this talk was never give before; it can never be given again—if God didn't do something spontaneous in me, both God and I would die of impoverishment of intelligence. That is why you never give the same treatment twice. You may treat the same person twice, and you may treat the same condition twice—indeed, one should treat it until it is right, if he can—but never twice alike. It is only as there is poured into this mold which thought makes—thought is the mold, but it isn't a creative thing in itself—a feeling which now springs into existence for the first time, that it is really a creative art, and treatment certainly is a creative art.

And we have to believe, then, that this creative process is still going on in us as us, and we should expect to see something new—every minute. We should never expect the same thing to happen twice alike. We should never expect life to descend into a monotony where there would be boredom. And it is an interesting thing that psychologically it is now known that the ennui of a lack of enthusiastic interest in life is what produces most fatigue in living. This has been well worked out in psychology: They call it "tired blood," but it is mental anemia really. It is a lack of an enthusiastic interest in life.

When you see someone who doesn't have any enthusiasm—life and enthusiasm, life and action—it has nothing to do with age, nothing to do with whether you are educated, or your intellect. It has to do with the need, the irresistible need, that the creative energy in the Universe shall flow through you, because it *is* you; and if you don't give it an outlet, all you will get out of that which is freedom is a congestion. So all congestion is creative, merely for the lack of an idea of flow—all of it—and all we have to do is to unthink the congestion. Constipation doesn't know it is constipation; it doesn't know it is anything, and it doesn't know anything. It only knows what is known about it, because it *is* what is known about it. And what it is and what is known about it are not separated from each other but are equal, identical, and interchangeable, just like the energy and mass of Einstein—it is the same thing. Therefore we attack it not in the sequence of its time track, subject to the law of its being—but previous to it, to set in motion a new causation.

And so freedom flows out of the same thing that produced bondage—there is no dualism anywhere. I know people who say, "I wouldn't do anything so materialistic as treat for an automobile." *I* would. They think they are getting around God or something they are still afraid of—and Jesus said to turn away from everything that looks like it. This isn't very easy to do, because the subject it images of the picture is in our own minds, and there is no difference between the picture and the thing. I always tell people, if they want money, to treat for it. The treatment is all right provided there is nothing in it that can hurt anything—you, someone; nothing that would hurt anything or coerce anything. The moment all those elements are taken out, is it not all right for an artist to paint a sunflower instead of a rose, if he wishes to? We don't fool the mirror; we can make up faces in it, and it makes them right back, and the only way to get a new reflection is to get a new image, and the only thing that

87

can change the image is its maker. And the only thing that can set a new sequence of involution in motion that will produce a new evolution that will produce a new situation is to start not with that which is already moving. We all do; and probably if we tune in somewhere, we help it out. But here is something we probably don't give enough thought to, it is so darned simple.

I know many people who say they will treat for substance and supply but not for money; but the subjective image is there, so that in treating for substance and supply they hope they will get some money. When they wanted wine, Jesus said This is the way to get wine; when they wanted money, he said Go and get that fish over there; when they wanted more fish, he said Cast your net there. There is nothing in the Universe that denies us anything unless that which we affirm denies the nature of the Universe in which we live, and if it does, there is nothing going to come back. If it came back, it would come back meagerly and for a very short duration of time—but that which affirms the Allness is the Allness affirming its own being. I don't think there is anything in the world that isn't all right to treat for. There might be some things that perhaps aren't worthwhile, in the light of a larger experience, but perhaps they are all right.

Is there anything big, little? The same energy that holds the Empire State Building in place holds a peanut on a table. It is an impersonal force operating upon everyone and everything: "He causeth the sun and rain to come alike to the just and unjust"; but we measure it out as good and bad, big and little, right and wrong—mostly as a projection of our own unconscious ideation, what is going on inside of ourselves.

There is a logic, a super-logic beyond all logic you and

I understand—a logic not based on the sequence of cause and effect, as our logic is. No matter how perfect our logic is, if the conclusion is based on a false or untrue conclusion to begin with—a wrong premise without departing from logic and mathematics—you can fabricate the most elaborate system that seems to be true, but is rotten at the roots. That is why Emerson said—and he certainly was not referring to me; but he was referring to us as a group, not consciously—we are the advent of that thing to which he looked forward, just as Jesus was not the Avatar or Messiah; the birth of the man Jesus was never prophesied in the Old Testament. It was prophesied by the Great Prophets that the time must come when the Thing they believed in should be incarnated somewhere, as It must and is still doing.

But Emerson said, Beware when God lets loose a thinker on this planet; then everything is going to be subject to change—everything. Why is that? Because a new premise is included. But most of our logic is built on the fact-fallacy of an inadequate premise; and philosophically and spiritually and theologically that false premise is dualism—not *dualism*, but a *belief* in dualism. No matter how subtle it is—and it creeps into New Thought and Christian Science and all these things—there is no such thing as a human mind and a Divine Mind. There is no such thing as a Universe divided against Itself. There is no such thing as dualism. There is no such thing as God *and* man—there can't be. There is only What Is and the way It works. There can be nothing in the Universe ultimately but action and reaction, the action being conscious intelligence and awareness, and the reaction intelligence unconsciously operating without an awareness.

Now let's treat for next Sunday's meeting, over in El

Monte, and where everyone comes to hear him* and receives the benediction of his consciousness and light of his awareness, love of his heart, intelligence of his mind, and companionship of his spirit in beauty, in joy, in happiness, in wholeness, in love, wisdom—and so shall everyone in that section know about this place, because even now we are acquainting them in the only Mind that exists, which is our mind, their mind, God's Mind—there is no other mind but this Mind.

Now let's treat to get rid of this smog in L.A.—to get back beyond all the arguments, back of everything to a time we all remember when it wasn't here, knowing it doesn't have to be here now—that whatever its cause may be, it can be ascertained and neutralized—and our word must find the outlet of that purity of atmosphere, that perfection which has always been associated with this remarkable country. And our dissipation of all this smog and fog in our own mind means that it is dissipated in fact. The word finds outlet in reality.

Let's know our President's message is listened to, realization of its reality is felt. Let's make it the law of our own being that we are happy, successful. . . .

*I.e. minister Ed Thompson.

CHAPTER 6

Dynamics and Analysis of Treatment

After dinner our custom was to watch several of Dr. Holmes' favorite TV shows—*Bonanza, Maverick,* and any of the people from Ernest's wide range of acquaintance making personal appearances. Following this we discussed people, I guess, for whom Ernest or I might be doing prayer work (Spiritual Mind Treatment).

I learned more in these talks than in studies, classes, and lectures. Dr. Holmes was patient and taught me that even though our work was teaching and practice, we often fell down in the practice, because we subconsciously doubted our authority to pray.

In March of 1959 Dr. Holmes gave one of his finest talks to the Tuesday Group on this subject. This was four weeks following the Feb. 12th Whittier Cosmic Consciousness Experience.

NOW LET'S TALK a little about analysis in treatment. What we believe in is practical, and I am particularly interested in the dynamics of our work. We collapsed the time in this El Monte church, less than 6 months, and I presented their charter last Sunday—shortest span of time we have ever accomplished this, I believe. And in presenting their charter, I said there are two things a Religious Science church stands for, and one is the recognition of the divine Presence, which of a necessity must be personal to each one of us, since it is personalized in us. And since no two persons are alike, it must be uniquely personalized to each individual, because it is individualized in each individual *as* that individual.

One of the things I think people in philosophic abstractions fail to realize is the inevitable necessity accompanying our teaching of a universality which is indivisible and in which we live—the inevitable, axiomatic necessity that even that which is universal must be intimately personal to that which it personalizes. It is a different concept, you know, than "the human down here and the Old Man up there." Did you see *Green Pastures* last night? I sat spellbound, but I didn't like the end, where the suffering came out. That is the morbidity which the human mind hasn't yet gotten over; the human mind is drugged with the concept of suffering as a divine imposition. It is intellectually and emotionally and psychologically drugged, because there is a certain morbidity about it that it loves to indulge in—like the old woman who said you could take all the weddings you want, but there is nothing so harrying as a good funeral. And she was right.

That morbidity is very well recognized in psychology, and that is why Freud said a neurotic thought pattern repeats itself with monotonous regularity throughout life —it is always morbid. People have these neurotic thought patterns—we all have them to a degree. If they are rather serious, they desire to be alone, that they may suffer with them. They become anti-social for the purpose of sitting on their fannies and feeling bad. This is true—it is not facetious; it is absolutely true. Now it is not because the real person wants it, but because the *neurosis* wants it. Rather interesting, isn't it? So much so that in all psychiatric work one of the first things is to separate the neurosis from the neurotic. Any good psychologist will tell you that it is not the neurotic but the neurosis who is talking. Mrs. Eddy called it error making a claim, and she was right. She said to separate the belief from the believer.

It is this thing that told Jesus not to cast the devils out of the pigs, etc. At the end of *Green Pastures* God said he has to suffer and they all have to suffer, and this is what goes back to the old theology—but the whole thing was beautiful. Now we all suffer and keep on suffering because we don't know better, but it is always the repetition of a thought pattern that doesn't belong to us— *invariably*. Suffering in and of itself can be neither person, place, nor thing—law, cause, medium or effect of itself—but it certainly sets up a big front and screams and argues, so that Jastrow* said one of the main troubles is what he called the inertia of thought patterns, which he said actually argued as though they were entities.

The neurotic likes to be by himself, that the neurosis may endlessly repeat itself; and it is always attached to certain definite experiences which now have no relationship to the apparent objective situation that causes it, but rather uses that upon which to play its familiar tune. It is always that way, practically, and recognized.

We have the concept of a divine Presence which is personal to us. That is the basis of all religions, all life—of everything—and believe it or not it is the basis of every man's reaction to life. I don't care who he is or where he

---

*Joseph Jastrow, American psychologist and author.

came from, what he does or what he believes, fundamentally at the root of all his concepts of life is his conscious or unconscious sense of relationship to the Universe in which he lives—whether he is at home in it and secure with it, or not. It doesn't matter who or what he is. As Emerson said, we have mistaken Jesus the man for virtue and the possibility of all men. Therefore we act endlessly as we do this week.* The whole performance of this week is foreign to my mind—I wasn't brought up in it. I could not crawl on the cross with Jesus on Friday and then crawl off it on Sunday. I just could not do it.

This whole idea of morbidity that goes with religion is based on a sense of insecurity, on a sense of not being at home in the Universe, not being wanted, needed and loved, not belonging. It is based on a completely dualistic concept philosophically, therefore it is based on a completely dualistic concept theologically (therefore a completely materialistic concept philosophically), and neither is compatible with modern physics—*neither*. You cannot reconcile very much: you can reconcile no philosophy of materialism or theology of dualism with the findings of modern science. That is why in the last 25 years, and last 10 and last 5—and it will increasingly accumulate—that is why scientific people of the last few years and of our day and who now begin to write on more than the technicalities of their science, begin to philosophize and begin, whether they know it or not, to accept the very position our philosophy is based on—infinite Intelligence acting as Law, and infinite Presence acting as Person. And this will increasingly accumulate until the need of man will be met in this field.

*I.e. Holy Week in the Christian liturgical calendar.

Arthur Compton* said that science has discovered nothing to contradict the concept of a universal Mind to which men are as its offspring—and that is interesting. He said materialism was 25 years behind the times.

Now we have this first concept; and the next one is the dynamics that go with it—and I think they belong together and should be taught together, whether we call it the law of Good that is greater than we are, which it is; or whether we call it the divine Principle, as Christian Science does, which is a good enough term for it; or whether we call it the universal Subjectivity as Troward did; or call it the Soul of the Universe, as it was originally taught; or the feminine side of nature, which receives the impress of the masculine and is impregnated with it and gives birth to creation, which is the immaculate Child; or whether we go with Plotinus and say there is a phase of Mind which is a blind force not knowing, only doing—it doesn't make any difference.

Because we are not only surrounded by divine Presence, which responds to us as Person—we are surrounded by a universal Principle, which responds to us as Law; and to this concept of Law we must add the concept of creative Intelligence without self-awareness, other than the awareness of what It is doing, not even knowing why It is doing it. That is why Plotinus called it a blind force not knowing, only doing. That is why Mrs. Eddy said, "Christian Scientists, be a law unto yourselves." That is why Jesus said, "The words I speak unto you, they are Spirit and they are Life. Heaven and earth will pass away, but *they* can't."

They have all recognized the universality of a Law which acts subjectively to, maybe not a higher Principle

---

*American physicist.

. . . but as a self-awareness which operates in It, around It, and through It—"The Spirit moved upon the face of the deep." We just call it the Presence and the Power and the Law, and that simplifies it and contains the whole works; and it is good to keep it simple. We believe in the Presence which we commune with, and the Law which we definitely use, consciously and concretely and for specific purposes. There is nothing wrong with this, there is nothing materialistic about what we call demonstration. If a person in a Christian theology would say there was, he would have to refute all the works of Jesus, because he based his whole authority on *what happened*—the whole thing. Jesus asked no authority other than *what happened* when he spoke his word. They asked, "By what authority do you do this?" and he said, "See what is going on." This is authority enough.

Now we believe in both, but we believe the finite mind, which merely is our use of the infinite Mind at a finite level . . . of course there is no such thing as a finite level, you know. Someone asked the other day, what is real of this and what is unreal, and I said, we do not deal with unreality, ever. There is no such thing as *what isn't*; there just can't be. We deal only with reality, no matter what face it shows to us. We know that even in reality there is an action and reaction which by the very law of freedom could temporarily bind us until we knew the difference between bondage and freedom; because if it couldn't, we wouldn't be free. We are bound by the cords of freedom, paradoxical as it sounds. If we weren't, we would be bound. That is why Annie Besant* said, "Karma is the law that binds the ignorant but frees the wise." The same

*English theosophist.

wind will blow a boat safely into the harbor or wreck it, depending on the way it is used.

Now I want to see a group of people . . . who if you almost have to beat them over the head with a club to make them do the few simple things that a group of people have to do to prove, as a group of people, what this group of people believe in. We have not exercised enough authority in our movement; and when I say that I shudder at my use of the word, because I am not talking about the authority of an organization, but the authority of something it uses. This is the new idea of authority we must introduce. It isn't my authority or yours. It is the authority of the thing we teach people, because it will never work very much other than on the basis of somebody recognizing its authority, will it? How can it? "My words fly upward, my thoughts remain below; my words without thoughts cannot to heaven go." The word is only a mold, a mechanical thing; the word is not a spontaneous thing, because it doesn't say itself. Therefore even the word has to be a reaction of the consciousness that generates it, doesn't it? "The words that I speak unto you, they are Spirit, they are Life." But some words are not very much alive!

At any rate, the word is a mold; but the thought, the feeling, the complete acceptance, the complete embodiment of what it does mean . . . when Jesus said, "Heaven and earth will pass away, but my words remain"—this was probably a literal statement. It seems to me if Lazarus hadn't come out of the tomb when Jesus told him to, Jesus would have had to crawl in with him and they would still be there. We cannot imagine an absolute affirmation knowing anything about even a relative denial, can we? That is why I think it is so important we realize that the human mind may not deny, even though it tries to. It may only affirm in two ways. If there were such a thing as the possibility of an absolute denial of the reality of the Universe, the Universe would be operating against Itself—do you realize that?—and science has found no energy in nature that will destroy itself. Jesus said, "If I do this by Beelzebub"—which is just a word picture, because he knew there wasn't any devil—"that wouldn't be good, because that would be a power divided against itself, and the world cannot operate that way."

Now these things we have to know; but just knowing them isn't enough. It isn't just enough for us to know God is Love—I mean it is a theory; if our arms are not around each other, how do we know God is Love? "Love only knows and comprehendeth love." Jesus said, "If you want to know about this doctrine, do it, and you will find out whether it is true; there is no other way." "Act as though I am and I will be"; "Be firm and you will be made firm"; "Believe and it shall be done," etc.

Now our conviction about the mechanics of things probably exists at the intellectual level and may exist at a feeling level; but if it exists only at intellectual level, remember this: a man with a good intellect may make a mold—and a perfect one mechanically, mathematically, with complete precision—but he wouldn't fill it with life. So in addition to that which he may mechanically do, there has to be a meaning; and there is no creative mold without a meaning—there just can't be; it is an unfertile seed.

So that feeling, I think, is something that while it will not deny the acceptance or rejection or analysis of intellect . . . the intellect may perceive, analyze, accept, reject, deny, affirm, and go through terrific performances until it builds an edifice or theoretical ladder from the earth to the skies; but it is a great question whether the intellect would ever climb the ladder, as such. *What* climbs the ladder, *whoever*, need not be repudiated by the intellect—is that clear? There is something else that goes with it. Now that something else that goes with it is really what is meant by the philosophy of mysticism, of intuition. It is a language of the feeling which, while it does not deny the intellectual conviction, sort of sweeps it up, adds warmth and color and feeling to it, which every artist will know as the difference between a technique and temperament. So the intellect may furnish a perfect technique, and I think it should—because if we have a science to teach, there is a principle involved, the way it works; it may be taught; a technique may be delivered and somebody use it, and we get a result. This I think we should never lose sight of, else there will be people running around looking kind of wild-eyed, saying, "This guy has such a terrific understanding; and when I get good enough or know enough or reach this point of exultation . . . "— you know what I mean; and such people never get any-place in our movement. They go on year after year, and after they have been in it for 40 years go back to a practitioner for treatment of a headache.

They don't quite seem to see: "I am the guy; this is it; this is the way it works; God speaks." I chose four subjects to use in June when I will speak for Carmelita:* God's Body; God's Business; God's Friendship; and God's Voice—as simple as that; arriving at the same thing. Now whether or not we call this a mystical concept, it will

---

*Carmelita Trowbridge, Religious Science minister (later, independent).

make a wonderful series, I think. Emma Curtis Hopkins*
is the best example of mysticism—metaphysical mysticism, as we understand it—as Plotinus is an example of
intellectual mysticism, too difficult; and of course Eckhart
and his mysticism is most beautiful of all to read. The
man who wrote this knew what he was talking about, it
is so darned simple.

Here is where a certain form of mysticism . . . but remember, mysticism is not mystery; mysticism is not psychism—it doesn't get hunches to sell this stock or where to
drill an oil well. That is psychism, and nothing wrong with
it—part of what is, part of the knowingness of the ever-
present Mind that put the oil there; and it can be done.
But I am talking about a transcendence, a something, a
feeling that is beyond thought. It is beyond analysis, beyond the possibility of the intellect's comprehending; yet
as I said last week at the close, this thing we are talking
about is something which the isolated intellect can neither
know nor comprehend, because it has not attached itself
to the concept of a liquid universe governed by flowing
laws which are intelligent—or as Emerson said, "We see
the universe as solid fact; God sees it as liquid law."

It would be inexplicable to the intellect and absolutely impossible for analysis, any kind of analysis, to take
mind beyond the threshold or that entrance to the thing
that is not explained but must be accepted. I would like
to cover that point, because a lot of people say, "After all,
you are getting us to a place where you go off the deep
end." This is one of the things the other psychologists ha-

---

*American religious metaphysician and mystic, New Thought
"teacher of teachers."

rangue against Carl Jung about—they say he has gone off the deep end of mysticism. He hasn't gone off any deep end at all. He just went to a place where they couldn't follow. But the strange thing is, every scientific research in the world does the same thing, but people don't realize it, through a process of analysis, or induction and deduction . . . because induction is only a series of steps of deduction—there is no such thing as induction and deduction in reasoning, any more than there is any such thing as affirmation and denial metaphysically; they are just different steps in the same thing. I think that is why Kettering* said that every invention is an intuition, and the progress of the invention in the development of its techniques is but a series of lesser intuitions. When you follow it out, it would have to be—because God cannot analyze but can only affirm. Therefore His language is yea and amen.

The mind—we will say the intellect—may conduct itself by a process to the doorway, gateway—Evelyn Underhill said there is a place in every person's mind that is this gateway—the gateway through which things inflood rather than outgo. Browning said, "It is Thou, God, Who giveth; 'tis I who receive." We are beneficiaries of the divine Fact. You and I didn't make the Universe; we may only accept It. We cannot even reject It. We may seem to; therefore it will appear to us in the form of our rejection —but it will appear in some form, from the lowest hell to highest heaven; and they are all made out of the same thing, because the lowest hell will become the highest heaven if you become harmonious there, and vice-versa.

Now the intellect may conduct the mind; they do this

*Charles Kettering, American electrical engineer and inventor.

in science. They say, Here is a principle, it will always work this way; and they don't try to explain it. But in religion and philosophy we try to explain everything that is inexplicable. This is one of the fallacies of theology and philosophy—I don't mean all theologians or all philosophers, but these people who run around and say what God's will is or what God's purpose is, or what God said, etc., etc.

The intellect, then, may lead itself just by cold-blooded reasoning, by mathematics. Pythagoras said it is all mathematics anyway. It may lead us to the place of the divine influx, but it won't cross that threshold through analysis. It is impossible, because here we get to the fact that the chicken lays the egg and the egg comes out of the chicken and the chicken out of the egg; and there is no rationality to it at all—doesn't even make common sense. Seen this way, there can be no such thing as life, because there is nothing to support it. Look everywhere you may and see if you will discover the song of the nightingale; dissect its body, etc. You just can never capture the song. It is just there; it is self-existent. Nothing made God.

So the intellect takes us to the place of acceptance. Now we want even more than this; we want the acceptance of not just a nebulous, theoretical Universe of possibility—and I don't really mean that, because if that were so, you would be conducting yourself to a Universe inane, inactive, unproductive; and you might fall again back upon your reason, which might even help out here a little, to help save something that is wrong—because there isn't a song. We will say there cannot be any such thing as an awareness that is not aware, there is nothing as an unexpressed life, there cannot be any such thing as a knower and have nothing known—there is no such thing as a Creator without a Creation.

Therefore, having arrived at the boundless possibility of limitless self-existence—inexplicable acceptance, even by pure mathematics—the logic is that something will have to happen to get beyond the threshold: something new, something wonderful—a new Creation. And so although we do not carry that which is explicable beyond the threshold of the inexplicable, we have not arrived at a place where nothing makes sense and it is all a vacuum and a dream. We have merely taken ourselves to the place where God sings a song—that is all—whether it is in the life of invention or whatever; but we have now reached a transcendence which no longer deals with the opposite, because it transmutes.

It becomes an affirmative language, and I think this is where we try to take our treatment. But now here we are coherent; we don't blubber; we are not incoherent. There is no God who is either praised or glorified by such inanities—not any kind. A God who has to be told He is a God is no kind of God, just like any person who is wrapped up in himself is wrapped up in a very small package; and it is all the same thing.

Here we merely venture forth into the boundless, into the limitless, into the possibility which is transcendent; but it will still be coherent. Right has to still express itself, and that is why even in modern psychology people like Kunkel* speak of the "unlived life." The creativity has to go on, and where it is refused outlet, it merely piles up the energy as alienation psychologically, because the

*Fritz Kunkel, psychologist.

conflict is always what is between the push here and the push back there. It is always in *here*; as Horney* said, always here at the center there will be four things—rejection, guilt, insecurity, and anxiety.

Now we want this dynamic thing to enter; but we would like it to *enter*: to feel noncombative, nonresistant, nonaggressive, in the sense of aggression against something that returns the aggression—"Who takes up the sword will perish by it"; might will be met with might, meanness with meanness. I got upset recently over several very little things: The first day I got fussed up over a little thing, then the next day something else happened just like it, and then another day something else just like it, and finally I said, "What's going on?!" I talked to myself about it. Emerson said imitation is suicide, over the doorway of consistency write "thou fool," and be a nonconformist—and all he was trying to do was to say, "Watch that spark in your own consciousness; you have something there—it is your only inheritance, because heaven and earth will pass away, but this thing won't. In talking to someone the other day, I said, "Let's forget that someone close to you and to me passed away and think of it in the broader viewpoint: When he arrived, the rest of us were here who were here. He got to the same place we came to, didn't he?—We all got to the same place when we got here. Find me one atom of logic that says we won't all get to the same place when we leave." If you are going to judge the future by the past, and the unknown by the known—it is as simple as that, isn't it? Browning said, "There won't anything be left out when God has made the

*Karen Horney, American psychoanalyst and author.

pile complete." I like this kind of thinking. Seneca* said, "Keep faith with reason, for she will convert thy soul." It will also help us out in every other way.

So we go back to this place where the Universe is now going to present itself for the first time to us in a unique way. We are not going to get on the other side of that gate and never do anything again. As the Universe abhors a vacuum, it is impossible for it to be inactive; but it is active, as Lao-tzu said, with an activity that seems inactive. He said all things are possible to him who perfectly practices inactivity, or inaction. Plotinus said, "When our face is turned to the One, our work is done better even though our back is to our work." That is mysticism. The Bible says, "Look unto me and be ye saved all the ends of the earth." They are all talking about the same thing—because it is only when we reach this place of noncombat, nonmonopoly, where no one has anything that takes anything away from somebody. . . . So I said to myself the other day, "Three things have happened, so you are messing around and meeting one thing with another." Either we free ourselves of these things or we are bound by externalities and there is no freedom, and nothing. So I asked myself, "What goes here?" and decided I better start a direction these things can't follow, because as long as they follow, they will have a story to tell—and we might look at it till we believed it. We have to get to a point of nondualism, noncombativeness, where there is nothing even to be saved or rectified or regulated, and for the first time we will arrive at the only place that can do all this, because in this nonresistive silence is the real affirmation

*Roman statesman, dramatist, and philosopher (4 B.C.?–A.D. 65).

and real action. All things are possible to him who can perfectly practice inaction. All action will flow out of that —like all voices will come out of the stillness or silence. So let's do it.

> *Now we are right here at this threshold where we are going to leave behind everything that says we can't step over. We are not going to take any of the darkness in with us, we are not going to take any troubles here, because there are no troubles this side of the gate. We are not going to take any impoverishment, fear, misunderstanding, or hurt—no patterns of antiquity that are repeating themselves over and over again just to show they have that much life. All this is behind us. This is what Jesus meant when he said, "Get thee behind me, Satan."*
>
> *And we know that where we now are, all joy exists, all perfection is forever. This is light, love, laughter, a song. It is peace; it is still. But here the most terrific action takes place we have ever imagined: Everything is alive; everything is awake, aware, whole; and everything is joy. Do we, then, drink from the well of salvation—the well which no man dug—and eat of the bread which no man made, and drink the wine which was not distilled—?*

CHAPTER 7

No Difference between the Prayer and What It Does

We don't hold thoughts, because creativity is immutable, and you can't stop that which is continuous and everlasting. In other words you can't hold the wind in your hand.

Relax and let it happen. Our attempts to force too much defeat us. The more you strain, the harder it is.

This talk of Nov. 18th (Thanksgiving time) 1958 enforced this conviction.

I sometimes think that Dr. Holmes bounced ideas off me for my reaction. I was under the impression that he thought that if *I* needed it, everybody else did.

WE ARE KNOWING the activity of the living Spirit within us, the one and only Presence, the All-Power operative now perfectly and permanently without effort, as we see it, known through us as the Law of our being or whatever we speak that word for, careless of the results because we are certain of them, with no burden or responsibility other than the knowing—knowing why we know what we know. We hold our mind to the perfect influx and outgo of absolute divine Intelligence, Law of order, Presence of peace and power, and the Essence of beauty. We know there is that within us which sees, knows, understands, and comprehends the meaning of itself, accepts it, without strain, without effort. And as we turn our thought to this church, this institution and all its branches and all the many phases of its activities, the word that goes out from it, whether written or spoken or on the air—we know that word carries with it the complete authority of itself, perfect realization of itself. Healing and wholeness go with it, and everything that every practitioner in this Movement prospers and heals instantly. Wherever this word is known, wherever it is spoken, the Law of its being is manifest in joy and harmony and love and wisdom.

Now we turn to our own consciousness—this thing which alone can, so far as we are concerned, be aware. We know it is infinitely aware; it is perfectly aware; it is permanently aware—all the Presence and all the Power there is in the Universe. Now let us establish in consciousness a church we are starting in El Monte—because this church stands for the conscious knowledge of the Presence, the power of perfection, of wholeness, of the manifestation of the living Spirit in Its own work, for God is not only in Creation, God is Creation—or else there isn't any Creation—and we are aware of this, we are establishing in our own consciousness a center to which everyone may come who needs help, who wishes to give help, a consciousness of love and beauty. We are establishing a thing of gladness and joy, and there is no weight, no burden, no heaviness, no past, no weariness connected with it. It is a song—a hymn of praise and a song of joy and a triumphant procession. It is a thing of beauty, of deep

feeling, of high vision and of laughter, of the silent communion of the soul with its source, and the outpouring
of the Spirit in its own Creation. Everything that we or-
dinarily would think, by a process of evolution shall un-
fold over a period of time we announce to be right now
and here, in this time and this place and today. All that
is ever to be, is; and it is going to be all that there is.
Therefore all that there is, is what it is right now, without
delay. That is good.

How many of you have ever read Emma Curtis Hopkins? You have to get the key to what she is talking about,
because it sounds screwy until you find out what she is
saying. But I suppose when Jesus said, "Behold the Kingdom of God is at hand," they all looked up and said, "The
man is crazy!" They didn't see what he was looking at.
They did look at what he was seeing. Now that is pretty
good; and it is true. They were all *looking at* it, and he
saw it. And I thought, Sunday—I was down in Mexicali;
we had been in Palm Springs and drove on down there;
it is the dirtiest place I have ever seen; I didn't know there
was anything like it anyplace; they seem to be very happy
people, more happy than we are; happiness is a different
thing than we think it is; you can't buy it—and I thought
to myself, where the vision is, there the Thing is.

This is the whole theme of Emma Curtis Hopkins' *High
Mysticism*: Where is the vision? Are you looking at a valley of dry bones or at mountain peaks and summits of
splendor and glory? Because wherever the vision is, there
is the imagery that molds the circumstances under which
we must live. And I got to thinking quite a bit about it,
because I was waiting for some people, and I thought,
"This is the way it will be while these people think this

way. They are not worse off than we are and we are not better than they are. This hasn't anything to do with big or little or right or wrong or round or square. There are no comparative things in the universe—there is no God that knows God is little in one place and big in another. The Universe itself knows nothing about good and evil— it only knows that It is; and what It knows, *is*; and what *is*, It knows; and Its knowing is the isness of what is. It is the law of its propulsion and the love of its impulsion, be- cause it is the givingness of the Infinite Self to Its self that it may experience Itself. Because if It experienced Itself without manifestation, It would remain in a dream state.

As long as there is a Creator, there will be a Creation. And as long as there is a Creation, there will be a Crea- tor in and as and through the Creation. It will be a mani- festation, but it will not be separate from what manifests. It won't be the Creator *there* and the thing *here*; and you will notice that in treatment, the treatment is the thing. The treatment is its own law, it is its own announcement, it is its own action. It is its own cause, its own effect. And it is its own whatever we call time, space, or anything in between. And the treatment contains everything that can ever come out of it—and nothing can ever come out of it that isn't in it.

That is what people do not understand about our sci- ence. When I say *our science*, it would be the same in Christian Science, Unity, and any of the New Thought or metaphysical movements. Most people think, "Well, holding thoughts is good." *The Power of Positive Think- ing* has had the biggest sale of any book in modern years, and it is a very good book and has helped millions of peo- ple—but it isn't what we teach. This is no criticism. I think this man is the greatest and is doing more good than anyone else in the nonmetaphysical field. But we don't sit around holding positive thoughts. You might say God doesn't say, "I will plant corn if it doesn't rain tomorrow," because God is the corn and the tomorrow and the planting and the harvest, and it all transpires in the Mind of God—and the Omega is in the Alpha. Psychology will say, "Well, suggestion is a very good thing for people"; but it isn't what we teach—because we don't suggest anything to anybody. And someone will say, "Yes, whatever you concentrate and set your will to, you can do." This has nothing to do with what we are talking about.

We are talking about two things only, which must suppose something back of them; perception supposes a perceiver, but we are talking about the perceiver and the thing perceived as being equal, identical, and interchangeable in exactly the same sense, I suppose, as Einstein said: Energy and mass are equal, identical, and interchangeable. He *did not* say that energy operates on mass; we *do not* say that Spirit operates on matter. He did not say energy operates *in* mass. These things are what he *didn't* say; he didn't say energy operates on it or in it—he said it *is* it; and if it were not it, mass and energy could not be interchangeable, could they? If the Universe is something other than a thing of thought or a movement of Intelligence, then there is no movement of thought or Intelligence that could affect anything in It—isn't that right? Our whole theory is based on the fact that the Universe is a *living* Universe, that it is an Intelligence operating as Law, that the Law of its operation is the movement of the Intelligence within It and upon It, *as* It.

Now if we arrive at that, there will be no difference between the treatment and what it does. The treatment will be what it does, and what it does will be the treatment and the doing—and they will be equal, identical, and interchangeable; and there will be no difference except one we don't see and one we do see—but what we do see is what we don't see as the prototype of what we do see.

Now this does not exist in any field other than our own —it would be impossible. Several of us were talking last night about how anyone can describe an experience unless he has had it. It is impossible. Shakespeare said, "He jests at scars who never felt a wound." Someone said, "Love only knows and comprehendeth love." Jesus said, "If you want to know the meaning of this, do it." Our motto is "To do is to know." They are the same thing— the doing and the knowing. Now no one understands us except people who are in our field. That doesn't exclude it, because thousands of people are studying to understand it, and they will; but unless they get the key to the whole thing—that, just as Einstein says, energy and mass are equal, identical, and interchangeable, which means they are the same thing . . . one is not opposed to the other, "approaching" or "receding from" or "evolving into" or "out of." *Equal, identical,* and *interchangeable!* You can turn energy into mass and mass into energy! Now this was exactly what Quimby* taught and what Mrs. Eddy taught, who were the forerunners of the New Thought movement—and I don't care who thought what or where they got it, because Truth doesn't belong to anybody, fortunately. What do we care what the Apostles wore? It is what they knew that matters.

As Emerson said, no kernel of grain can come to us unless we plant it and harvest it—the immediate Thing in

---

*Phineas Parkhurst Quimby, American inventor, religious philosopher, and mental healer.

our own consciousness, because each one has to do It and be It for himself; because he is It, but he doesn't know he is It. Therefore he is like a fish swimming around in the sea looking for water because he has heard of it, and he doesn't know it is running through his gills, and that he is in it and derives his life from it. So "In Him we live and move and have our being."

I was thinking, Sunday, if all we thought about was mud flats, we would be living on mud flats. Now maybe we would be just as well off. I am not talking about the comparative degrees of social order, because I don't know that it makes any difference. There is nothing beyond happiness—and if you can be happy in a mud puddle, you are better off than you are being miserable on a throne. As someone said, a half of something is better than three-fourths of nothing, and I am sure it is true.

But, I thought, *it is certain wherever the vision is set*— because here are a group of people who at least, when it rains, can put a little sand in the front yard and not walk through a pool of water to get to the street. Now if this law applies, we are all in some kind of a mud puddle, aren't we? and sitting beside some kind of a stream that is stagnant. And so the comparison has nothing to do with looking down our noses and saying, "Thank God we are not as other men." I suspect that the average person there is as happy as the average person in L.A. The question is: Couldn't he be happy without the mud puddle? If he couldn't, I am all for his having it, because it is all relative anyway, and no one knows what is good and what is bad. The ones who think they know so much about it are evangelists.

Now there is nobody any more screwy than they are— because their dualism is something terrific, and the evil that goes with it; but that is their vision. Hell will never cool off until people get cooled off. Emerson said he went out into a field after a hot political meeting and nature seemed to say to him, "Why so hot, little sir?" And in one of Shakespeare's plays—I think it happened in *Romeo*—he is a little guy and says, "A little pot soon boils."

I saw there, and thought, *they are just as well off as I am; I don't think I would like it this way; they wouldn't like it the way I have it.* The comparison is not that they are socially inferior or intellectually inferior. I don't know that they are. Some of wisest people I have ever known have very little intellectual training—but they seem to know about something that the intellect is often offended by if we try to coerce it to believe. As a matter of fact, intellect, as much as we need it, we have to stretch consciously that it may become aware of that which is superior to it—even to get enlightenment.

I think there is a soul-touching and intellectual process that stretches the intellect through the imagination and feeling until it lets in more spiritual territory, which now becomes a part of the intellect. And I cannot conceive that we reach a place where chaos is and we don't have any intellect or intelligence. I don't think we push out into the Universe to the loss of identity. I think we merely take in more territory, and more, and more. "Ever as the spiral grew, he left the old house for the new."

But here is the whole theme of *Where is our vision set?* Now particularly in treatment, because we discussed this quite at length . . .and from someone who is supposed to know nothing about it, other than as a sweet "believe-it-is-so," I got some of the most profound wisdom I have ever listened to—isn't this amazing: you never can tell where you are going to learn and from whom—and an absolutism that was perfectly amazing. You never can tell what people are thinking about when you see them in ordinary life. You think probably they are pretty far from what you are—and you like to think your own exalted thoughts, which you find aren't so exalted when you come to analyze them and wonder how you got that way yourself. But it really gave me a very interesting slant on the absolutism of relativity. Because if there is an absolutism beyond relativity—which there is—we don't yet know it, and even that which we postulate as absolutism, is reached through relativity. And if the reaching out isn't the thing that it reaches—if it isn't the thing that is reached after and with—then if our hand touched it, we wouldn't recognize it; it would look unfamiliar and we would throw it in the river. We wouldn't understand it.

Now Jesus said, "Behold"; he saw what he was looking at; *they* were looking at what he saw but didn't see it: "Eyes have they but they see not." Jesus said, "Behold"; and they looked up and said, "The guy is screwy; he sees nothing, because there is nothing there, and we don't see it either. And because we don't see it, it isn't." Now his vision was tuned into something that he saw, so what he was looking at, he saw; what he was looking at, *they* looked at and did not see. That is all the difference. Where is our vision set?

Now Troward said—and he is by far the best writer in this field; about half my stuff comes from Troward; the other half came from wherever I could pick it up; what is left over I made up, because by then I knew it didn't matter who made it up, because it was all made up anyway; sort of like our discussing very elaborately this morning whether we should try onions and celery to put in the turkey dressing—Troward said: in such degree, in treatment, as we believe that our treatment is conditioned by the past, the present, or the future, we are not treating in what we might call the realm of the absolute, or let us say the realm of unconditioned causes. I like "the realm of unconditioned causes" better than "the realm of the absolute," because it means more to me. It isn't any better.

The realm of unconditioned causes: that which all of effect must come from, and upon which effect must depend, but which itself does not depend upon effect. Therefore, the effect would be the plaything of the cause. Relativity is the plaything of the absolute, in a sense. But our treatment and what it is going to do would depend on where we condition it, and we shall condition it wherever our vision is. "And he went up into a mount and when he was set, his disciples came unto him and he opened his mouth and taught them, saying Blessed are the pure in heart for they shall see God." He didn't say that other people wouldn't see. He said there is a divine vision; that no matter what it looks at, it will see through what Swedenborg called the exteriors into the interiors—through an interior awareness—and it will see God, because it will see what it is looking at; but all people will be looking at it and not see what it is looking at. Now we believe there is a vision, mental vision, which looks away from what doesn't belong, and looks at the place that does, according to where the spiritual vision is set—in the realm of unconditioned causes, then, Troward said. This is what we are dealing with. Whether or not we are aware of the fact, we are still dealing with it; and what it shall do for us will not depend upon it, because what it does for us is a reaction of what we have done, not *to* it, but *in* it.

I was explaining to a young fellow this morning—young producer at one of the studios. He was working so hard, and I said, "Larry, you don't force anything, you don't coerce anything, you don't hold any thoughts, you don't put in anything—you always take it out. Always. It is already in there." His mind was all burdened with things he has to do. He has a great responsibility, and he was making it a personal thing—he had to make things happen. Now is the time to relax, I told him; we take everything out. And he said, "Then what makes it happen?" I said, "It is like you put the acorn in the ground, that is your part. Now there is an idea involved in that; and nothing can happen to the idea but that it will grow, and nothing can stop it but its own law. It is its own evidence; the oak tree is already there. You put an idea into your mind, and it will work exactly the same way, because the Universe is one system."

"Well," he said, "then I don't have to strain"; and I said, "No, the more you strain, the harder it is going to be." There is a certain relaxation. The realm of unconditioned causes is also the realm of Einstein, I am sure—of pure energy, before the action takes place which causes it to become mass (but it can turn itself back into it).

Now suppose we had a bottle of liquid and you could turn it into a mold and it would become a human body—have all the action a human body has. But now something has endowed it with intelligence also; and then suppose, theoretically, you could turn the body back into the bottle, and as you turned it it would become liquid again. You would know that objectivity and subjectivity are equal, identical, and interchangeable; but you would know there is something beyond both. This, of course, Einstein didn't philosophize on—a something that had

117

will, had volition, had life, had self-determination, and which discovered that energy and mass are two sides of one thing which may be liquid or solid; but when it is the one it is the other, and when it is the other it is the one.

Einstein himself stood above this with his equations, separate from the thing he was equating, in a sense— didn't he? At least let's say, he manipulated it: he turned the liquid into the form and turned the form into liquid. Quimby did the same thing a hundred or more years ago. He said that mind is matter in solution, and matter is mind in form; but he said they are the matter of Spirit. In other words, he had a third thing he postulated there, which uses mind, whether it is liquid or solid. Mrs. Eddy said disease is the image of thought that appears in the body. They are saying the same thing. Emerson said, "We see the universe as solid fact, God sees it as liquid law." This is the basis of our whole work—that consciousness establishes its own form independently of any form that is already established, but only when it has a new impulsion or idea or vision in the realm of unconditioned causes. We live in the realm of absolute cause, which is causeless, but which causes everything, within itself; whose sole and only action can be upon itself; and whose sole and only reaction can be the reaction of itself to itself, making out of itself that which it presents to itself for itself in itself.

I like always Aurobindo's* thought, as he says, "for the delight of God." I have never anywhere heard a more beautiful expression of the mystical meaning of creation: he said it exists for the delight of God. Nothing has ever

*Sri Aurobindo, Indian seer, poet, and nationalist.

satisfied me as much, because now we know that where there is an inhibition of that creative stream, all of the psychological liabilities occur which psychiatry and everything is working on. We know that.

Well, then, if we had this kind of an energy and mass and somebody to turn it back and forth . . . now it wouldn't do any good if Einstein just arrived at the equation; he said, Boys, go out and do it this way and turn it back and forth, explode it and see what happens—that is the way they got the atom bomb. Tennyson said, "appearing when the times were right"—but not a good thing for the world, as we see it now; maybe it will be. It is as good as we make it.

But Quimby understood that there is a "superior wisdom," which he called Christ, and the use of it, which he called the science of Christ. One of his whole sayings was on the nature of man and another on the science of Christ. That is where scientific Christianity comes from; because he said the relationship of this thing which holds the visible and the invisible in its hand—I am putting this in my own terms—is the relationship of something superior to both the liquid and the solid, to which the liquid and the solid are the matter of wisdom.

Both the word and what the word does are products of the thing that speaks the word. He called this a divine wisdom and a superior wisdom. He said, "I represent this man of wisdom, and I enter your opinions and I explain why they are, and I explain away the solid fact," which in this case was disease. Mrs. Eddy went way beyond him but this is very interesting on its simpler basis. He said, "I explain away the solid fact, and it liquifies; and you ask me, what is my cure, and my answer is: my explanation is my cure." Jesus said, Know the truth and the truth shall make you free. Psychiatry says, Bring it to the light of day. But we go way beyond that.

Jesus always operated from the absolute position of the unconditioned in the realm of unconditioned causes, without reference to the past or present or future—"Who was born blind, this man or his parents? and who did sin when he was born?" Now Jesus paid no attention to it. He didn't say, Let's discuss the theory of the Jews, or Let's discuss the theory of the Hindus. They were both good people. They knew of only two contracts—grandfather to grandson; incarnation and reincarnation. They couldn't imagine anything else. He steps right out into the emptiness of spiritual space and says, Three cheers for God! I have a new one! That is all that happened; we don't have to get sanctimonious. Jesus knew something which he called the truth, which was acquainted with freedom—I Am—and he knew it in his own consciousness and nowhere else. And that is where you and I will have to know it.

And so just as Einstein and the scientist and the physician "stand superior" to manipulate the energy and mass of their doubt, so Quimby said there is a superior intelligence that does, and will, mold and remold that part of nature which is matter as form and mind as liquid form; and matter as form is more solid than mind, and mind as liquid form is a little more juicy than matter. But they are the same thing—they are equal, identical, and interchangeable.

Now if we are living in such a universe, then we get back to the mystical concept that I started with; this is the mechanics which react to the concept. Now these mechanics will always be there, but they are always covered up and always hidden. In other words, if things work the way in which they work, that is the mechanics of the universe; and it is either Jachin or Boaz—either that one of the two pillars in front of the Temple of Solomon that stands for the law, or the other one, which stands for the word or spontaneity. Every form is liquid, every form is transparent, every form contains a light which can be seen, every form responds to the language that addresses it with a consciousness of union with it, from the lowest to the highest forms of life—from the mind that sleeps in the mineral, waves in the grass, awakes to simple consciousness in the animal and self-consciousness in man and God-consciousness in the hierarchies in which I believe. But I don't believe in them in the sense of masses that are controlling us. I am talking about the upper hierarchies of intelligence manifesting through instrumentalities which have now arrived at a perception of the meaning of intelligence—because in Jesus it automatically flowed; he saw it and therefore it was. When we see it, it will be; but see how we are conditioning everything we do. Now that means that while our treatment creates and deals with process, in a sense, all process that we add to it is inherent in the Law, and the word is superior to the Law. As Troward said, you start with Absolute Intelligence, then word, then law, then thing. But it is only up here in Absolute Intelligence that we come into the realm of unconditioned causes, because there are absolute causes and there is the Absolute as cause, and there are any number of variations of relativities that become the absolute to that which is relative to them. Right down the line.

Emerson said that we awaken with consciousness that we are on a certain step, and we know there are steps above us and below us—Jacob's ladder—which intuition perceives; so there are any number of relative causes— and any relative cause that we stop at, we make it temporarily an absolute cause to that which is relative to it. In other words, it controls it. It governs it. If we believe we are subject to planetary influences, we will become subject, not to planetary influences, but to whatever subjective and psychic belief the world has created relative to what they think it does. If we believe that there are devils, we will be subject to some kind of satanic influence, which has no existence outside of human beings, which will be commensurate with the sum total which all people believe it to be who have believed in it and still do. "The devils also fear and tremble."

If we believe that we are subject only to the law of harmony, we shall harmonize, at present, with what is the top level of what the uniform concept of harmony is. I think if we broke the bonds of the lesser, we would be like a balloon where all the ballast is thrown out. I don't happen to believe anybody would stay in this world if he got rid of all the things that keep him here. Now I am not saying whether it is desirable to come or go; I don't know and don't care. I think we still have considerable weight around our neck—and I haven't seen anybody who has loosed it. Every bondage we subject ourselves to, we automatically in our vision subject ourselves to the mathematics of that bondage. We are tied. Jesus said of Lazarus,

"Loose him and let him go." And we have to be loosed before we can go. If our thought must be in the realm of unconditioned causes, still, when it comes to treatment, our believing that there is anything other than action and thought will lead us to the diagnosis.

Now this is what they do not understand in psychosomatic medicine. I know I believe in medicine, I believe in surgery. If we could get our vision beyond all these things, we could sleep without a pill; and while we sleep with the pill, we are subject to the harm that the drug does to the human body and mind, which knocks out both body and mind.

Every form of conditioning which we give our treatment does not condition the principle; it makes the relativity of that principle equal only to the conditioning which is being imposed upon it. Now this doesn't imply that it has any bondage, or that it is caught, or that it is evil or limited. The very fact of its freedom proclaims a necessity of this thing we call its bondage to us, because that is the only way we look at it; and I think we shall have to see that bondage is freedom, else we will be struggling with another set of dualisms. Freedom *and* bondage —this cannot exist. And we shall be trying to lift our consciousness to a point of perception, not of freedom as opposed to bondage, or the destruction of bondage as opposed to freedom, but of action without restriction. Just action. This is the way it is.

Therefore every treatment must have that tint of absoluteness in it, in the mind of the one who gives it—it doesn't matter whether anybody else knows anything about it—and it is arrived at in such degree as one is able mentally and theoretically to let go of everything even that the treatment has to get rid of. That is rather interesting, isn't it? Now 90 percent of all healings and demonstrations are made through a process, a mental process of arriving at this, but I don't wish to imply that I am thinking of a divorce of the absolute from the relative—there is no such thing as a relative separate from the absolute or not proclaiming the absolute. The slightest relativity proclaims the absolute at the level of that relativity. I struggled for a number of years to knock the relativity in the head with the absolute—and the only thing that got knocked out was myself, and I realized I didn't have strength enough to fight the Universe. That nonviolence, that flexibility, that acquiescence, if you will, walks with you. "And whosoever shall compel thee to go a mile, go with him twain"—what is it that makes you walk two? That is what Jesus was talking about.

In other words, Jesus knew there was no combativeness in the Universe. He knew there is no dualism, he knew there is no something else—there is only one end. And so if our treatment is to be absolute—it is going to be absolute anyway—but if it is going to function in *the realm of unconditioned causes* (which is why I like that expression) or if it is going to transcend the condition, or change the condition, it has to rise above it to the point where it sees either the *completion* of the one or the *process* of the other one. Either one will do it. As you hold a piece of ice in your hand, it melts. The process is *holding the ice in your hand*, and there is nothing wrong with the process, because it tends to the clarification of thought into manifestation of the thing thought about.

So I have been thinking about that, even down there
the last two or three days—kind of engaged my thought;
and driving through the mountains and the desert, always
I was trying to figure out in my mind what does *the realm
of unconditioned causes* mean to me? I don't know what
it means to you; you don't know what it means to me;
but I do think in the interchange of thought we very frequently get it clarified, and it means more to each other.
I believe very much in the psychic communion between
groups and between people—that something is set up;
they call it darshan in India: a relationship which, flowing out from the group and the individual, reaches a little higher altitude and flows back into the group and the
individual, more rarified.

In other words, if anybody gave a talk to an audience
and helped the audience, it would have to help him. If he
gave a talk that depressed the audience, he would have
to be worse off for having given it. Anyone who talks a
lot about hell in his sermon will be more deeply in hell afterwards. I don't say this as condemnation. Everybody
has a right to be in hell or he wouldn't have created it. But
he would be more deeply immersed in it.

Now it is hard for us not to talk about morbidity, isn't
it? I thought when I looked at those guys: my God, it is
terrible—how can they do it? Then I thought, it is home
to them, it is where they live, where the kids are playing*;
they are probably happier than we are. Therefore it is to
the interior of the thing and not to the exterior that we
have to look—to the feeling of it. (But I did leave that

*I.e. Mexicali. See p. 109.

125

place very gratefully.) And let's see if we can't do that in our own mind and awareness.

To become conscious that we are manifesting, that we are existing, we are speaking, we are thinking in the realm of unconditioned causes where reality makes a thing out of itself by becoming the thing that it makes, and that we now turn to it—"Come to me and be ye saved": that is what it means; "Looking up they beheld his face only": that is what this means; when Moses came down from the mountain his face shone: it all means the same thing—it has no reference to a physical altitude; "I will look up unto the hills from whence cometh my strength": same story as *Pilgrim's Progress*—"As he reached the top the burden fell off and rolled away": it is the mind no matter what age is perceiving—that there is an altitude of thought where the eye views the world as one vast plane and one boundless reach of sky: that is what the poet said; he is telling the same thing Jesus did and all of them, probably through intuition, inward feeling, a witness of the soul; He has never left Himself without a witness.

And we do perceive the wonder of it all, and we do accept the wonder of it all—and *all* of it, right here and right now. And so it is.

PART II

CHAPTER 8

Cosmic Consciousness Experience: February 12, 1959

Dr. Holmes spoke at the Dedication of Christ Church of Religious Science, Whittier, California.

At the time, the minister was Rev. Reina Lady Smith. She also was a good friend of mine. President of the Board of Trustees of the Whittier church was William Hart, a friend of more than thirty-one years.

That evening Dr. Holmes experienced what has been accepted as a Cosmic Consciousness experience. He kept me up most of the night talking about it, telling me I must never tell anyone what we discussed.

Thanks to Reina and Bill, I was given a seat in the space over the platform where an immense immersion baptismal tank had been removed. This furnished me an ideal vantage point to look down on the platform and Dr. Holmes while he was speaking.

That night he told me he had the sensation of being at the roof of the Church looking down at himself talking. I asked him what he saw. He said, "The whole church and people there became a pool of light." When he left the podium, he stumbled momentarily as though with an effort the man on the roof was forced back into the man at the podium.

Following the address of February 12, note in particular the talks of January 27 (two weeks before this address) and February 10 (two days before the address). Both talks were given at the meetings of the Tuesday Invitational Group.

After February 12 there were three Tuesday Invitational Group talks on healing work (Feb. 24, Apr. 14, and Apr. 28). Note the vein of the talks, reflecting the Whittier Experience.

Rev.Reina and Bill Hart gave me a cassette tape of the talk after it had been transferred from the disk of the old Grey Autograph that had been used to record Dr. Holmes' talk.

["This is William Hart speaking. We are privileged to bring to you Ernest Holmes' Dedicatory Address at Christ Church of Religious Science, Whittier, California, on the night of February 12th, 1959.

"The occasion is notable because Dr. Holmes experienced the greatest illumination of his lifetime during this talk. The tension of the moment is clearly discernible in the changing quality of his voice as the talk progressed.

"There were present on the platform that evening, in addition to Dr. Holmes, Drs. William H. D. Hornaday, Mark T. Carpenter, Barclay Johnson, Reina Lady Smith (the local minister), and the local Board President, which position I then held. In the congregation were over 400 persons, with a small overflow listening to loudspeakers in the basement.

"Sitting behind Dr. Holmes, I could not see his expression during his experience, but I am told by others that his face was really radiant. When he turned from the podium to retake his seat on the platform, he appeared physically debilitated and emotionally overwrought. He quickly regained his composure, however.

"During the reception which followed the dedication, I learned from Mrs. Smith that Dr. Holmes had told her briefly of his experience but was hiding it from the congregation for fear that it might be misunderstood. As soon as the situation permitted, Doctor Holmes went home, chauffeured by his friend Dr. George Bendall. At a much later date Dr. Bendall told me that Dr. Holmes, with whom he was living at the time, kept him up a good part of the night discussing the experience.

"We apologize for the poor quality of the tape. The original recording was made on a borrowed Grey Autograph—an early stenographic device that recorded on a plastic disk. The voice was then transcribed to a home-type phonographic record and later placed on modern tape. The original recorder was concealed in the lectern which Dr. Holmes was using. He leaned often against the lecturn, causing it to squeak and groan. Unfortunately, the recorder was at times more responsive to the extraneous noises than to the speaker's voice. The next voice you hear will be that of Dr. Ernest Shurtleff Holmes."]

I HAVE THE keenest personal interest in such an occasion as this, and the most impersonal interest, in that I love it personally, and I don't feel that it has anything to do with me at all, other than that it is a certain phenomenon which is taking place in my day and which I have the privilege of being some part of. Tolstoy in "War and Peace", which is still called "the best six novels ever written," by all the writers, said that any person today who appears to do anything worthwhile, probably has the least of anyone of his age to do with it.

He is merely something—an instrumentality—that the principle of evolution probably leaves upon the shores of time to see what'll happen. If it happens, he has the opportunity of being one who appeared to help. If it doesn't happen, he and it go out on the next tide, because only that which persists in evolution—finally, that which is worthy—can remain. As Tennyson said, "So careful of the type it seems, so careless of the single life."

Our movement grows and expands very rapidly—as rapidly I think as is possible—because we would not wish to mistake its end and purpose, which is not the building of churches. It is not the dedicating of churches—it is what happens in them after they are built, and after they are dedicated. It's what happens where there are groups of people in our conviction who meet together for the only two purposes for which we exist—teaching and practice. We have many orators in our midst, such as Barclay Johnson and Bill Hornaday and others here—but that isn't enough. What happens? For, as Shakespeare said, "A man may smile, and smile and smile, and be a damnèd villain still."

So we could profess and confess and exclaim and proclaim that God is all there is, and no one would believe us; unless something happens when we say it.

We are a teaching and a practicing order in the Christian Faith, who believe in two great fundamental realities —the Divine Presence, personal to every living soul and uniquely personal to each and every one of us. That's the first great cornerstone. The next is a Power for Good, and the Law of Good in the Universe greater than we are, that we can use for definite and specific purposes. The first one, everyone believes in. The second proposition, probably about twenty million people in this country now believe in, somewhat. And that two hundred thousand of them really know what it is that they believe—I doubt it.

It is our endeavor, through our educational system, to teach people what this principle is, and how to use it.

And there is a growing conviction in my mind that it should and must become the endeavor of all of our leaders to exercise some kind of a discipline over their membership not as to their theology—because I'm the world's worst theologian. I don't even know who wrote the books of the Old Testament, and I'm sure I don't care. I don't know what kind of underwear the Apostles wore, but I'm sure it's worn out! and most of their other beliefs are, too. They did not have electric lights or automobiles. They didn't know how to make pancakes, and I doubt very much that they had very much understanding of what Jesus had taught them. That is not our endeavor, to convince somebody of our faith. It is to *prove* something— first of all to ourselves; then to the world—and we have no authority before the world, and should ask for none— and will have none, *ever*—I hope—other than the authority of the work that follows the word. Should we become the most prosperous organization in the world, and build temples that would make Taj Mahal jealous and blush with shame . . . we should have become the most dismal failure in the entire history of the evolution of man's concept of God. It is not at all strange that the time should have come and it happened to come in our time; and we happen to be those through whom and to whom it came. How fortunate we are!

How lucky you and I are that we are here tonight. Oh, we are indeed favored among all people on earth of all ages. Why, we have taken the banner that Jesus resigned when he said to the thief beside him, "Do not be afraid. Today shalt thou be with me in Paradise." It is quite a banner. It is with this banner that we advance, and advance from chaos and the night.

We are a teaching order, not a preaching order. We are a practicing order, not a proselyting order, and the world has waited long and too often vainly for something to happen; for some healing power of the unseen magic of the Spirit to be evidenced at the cornerstone. . . .

When I was a kid I knew people who even had oxen— it's a long time ago. I did meet somebody down at Johnnie Hefferlin's church last night and he said he admired me very much, and he said, "You are so much like another friend of mine. He is ninety-two." And I said, "Well, I'm still holding my own. And as long as I don't slip backward, everything's going to be great."

But I had something stirring inside of me—what they call a restless foe. I would like to get one thing done without getting another started that's a little bigger than the other thing, else you *are* slipping back.

You know, we haven't yet done what I believe we should do with our membership. Now we're here tonight to dedicate a church, a physical building. I think it's beautiful, I think it's wonderful. I think it's a miracle, but I know why it is here. It's here because you're here, and because Dr. Reina Smith is here; and because your consciousness and hers and Bill's and all of you wonderful

134

people out here have cleaved together, and what happened? Power—like the weaving of a rope, where one strand will hold no weight, but united it will hold terrific weight.

We have yet to see what the multiplied consciousness of a church body can do, if they are properly trained, if they permit someone to exercise an authority over them —not of their theology for which I wouldn't give a nickle anyway, not of their private lives which are no one's business but their own, but of one thing only—there is a Law of Good. There is a Power in the Universe greater than we are and we can use it; and it will multiply its effects a thousand times, in my belief, through the united consciousness of a group.

I have had so much inward conviction about this the last year—and the members of the Ministerial Association know about it—that I know, as I know that I am here, that you, right here, under the leadership of your most inspired leader, who has balanced the human and the divine equation, so that God and man unite on earth—*you* are going to prove this. Others will. I know that *you* will —because of what's happened here. Let me tell you this: it is the only excuse we have.

There are many wonderful religions in the world. We are not better than the others. We are not more spiritual. We are not more evolved. We are not more anything, other than this one thing: we have co-joined our consciousness with the eternal verity of the Universe, that that everlasting and eternal Father of all life, and the Mother of all creation forever begetting the Only-Begotten, is begetting Him in us, right now. And that the word of our mouth is a word of Truth in such degree as it emulates and embodies the Truth which sanctifies the word to its unique service of healing not only the sick, but the poor in heart.

We are dedicated to the concept that the pure in heart shall see God—here; that the meek will inherit the earth —now; that one with Truth is a majority; that every one of us, in the secret place of the Most High, with center on his own consciousness, has the secret with the Eternal, the Everlasting, the Almighty, and the Ineffable: God and I are One. And I see you doing this; and I see you uniting in one great hymn of praise, one great union of effort, one crescendo of song, and one enveloping light of consciousness . . . [long pause]

I see it! [longer pause]

O God . . . the veil is thin between. We do . . . mingle with the hosts of heaven.

I see it.

And I shall speak no more.

[At this point, witnesses agree, Dr. Holmes seemed to stagger slightly, and he returned to his chair. The event was not disclosed nor was it committed to writing until eleven years after Dr. Holmes' death on April 7, 1960.]

CHAPTER 9

Treatment Clarifies Thought

W<small>E START IN</small> Santa Monica next Sunday morning. I want all of you to work every day this week for the right consciousness and a full house next Sunday morning at Santa Monica. Few people realize that all in the world a treatment is is a conviction or belief you put in your own words, and that the Universe is made out of words. This is the most difficult thing we have to believe and yet it cannot be any different in our field than Einstein's concept of energy and mass being equal, identical, and interchangeable. Our whole theory is based on the concept that there is no difference between the thought and what it does, there is no difference between the thought and the form it takes. Because how could thought change a form unless form were thought as form? It just couldn't. That is the whole basis of our treatment.

Let's treat that. I'll show you how I treat it, and this is the way I would like you to treat it every day this week:

We are speaking definitely and specifically for this particular location, Santa Monica Bay Women's Club the next four Sundays, and after that right along. Certain notices have gone out; they will be in papers. People have spoken about it, telling each other about it. And we know that place will be full and running over, that every person who has received this notice whom we can benefit will be there. Every person who has been told about it who can be benefited by being there—we don't want him to come if he can't—will be there. Every person who reads about it who can be benefited by being there will be there. We know there is a consciousness of healing, a consciousness of wholeness and happiness and well-being, a consciousness of love and friendship and unity and security and peace, which everyone feels and knows and understands, because it belongs to everyone.

Now we know that as people sit there they find themselves healed of all unhappiness, of all sorrow, of all grief, of all loneliness, of all confusion, of all doubt. This word which we now speak is present and active in this group, doing and being and accomplishing and becoming exactly what is in our mind now, because we speak it for a definite place, a definite location, a definite time—the only time and place there is in the Universe which is the one we place in time, so far as we are concerned. Therefore it operates at this time; it cannot fail to operate; it is present, active, healing, renewing, vitalizing, filled with goodwill and good cheer and love, and filled with beauty and harmony. It embraces this audience in light. And that is the way it is.

Last Sunday there were about twice as many in Santa Monica as usual because of the work we had done. And last night I had a meeting of the Board of Santa Monica Trustees—and Don Fareed* is president of the Board—

---

*Son of Ameen Fareed, M.D., popular and renowned psychiatrist, who frequently wrote and spoke for the Religious Science movement.

and they were telling me how they could feel a movement. It is interesting, isn't it? The most interesting thing in the world to me is to find some definite action taking place in what appears to be outside of us, as a result of what we are doing inside of us; and I don't see that we would have any evidence that what we are doing is real, unless something definite does happen out there. We would, I think, soon just be mumbling words without meaning. We have no evidence whatsoever that what we believe is true, outside of what it does.

As you know I am on the radio with Bill [Hornaday] twice a week for awhile on questions and answers, and I said last week, "There ain't no hell." Someone might have written back and said, "The hell there ain't!" Someone did write and said, "Dr. Holmes may think there isn't any hell, but he will find out!" Isn't it strange how difficult it is for people to give up their sadism, and every pit of it is a projection of their own unconscious sense of guilt. If this sweet soul could cool off hell for herself, she would send me to heaven gladly. Wherever she is, she is a sweet person and she would like to save me. How strange it is that the human mind is so morbid and so afraid and so cluttered up with confusion that it doesn't think straight.

Someone told me just last night—one of the Board members, who was interested in the youth movement and having a party—that one of them said to this person, "You will either have to give me an aspirin or a treatment," and she said, "Well, I don't carry aspirin, so I can't give you that, but I carry treatments with me; so now let's all get together"—there were about sixteen girls there, about 16–17 years old—"and let's remember that treatment is clear thinking; and we will think clearly." And before they got through thinking clearly, the girl said, "Well, it is all gone!"

Now this could not happen unless whatever transpired in the consciousness of those who were working produced that effect, because we no longer suppose we sit here and pray to a God up there to do something over there. When this happens and something over there is done, it is measured out over there at the level of the acceptance and embodiment here in a field of unitary wholeness. We have a lot of practitioners in this group, and they come from different groups, many New Thought movements; and we all think exactly alike when it comes to treatment, as far as I know. We learn in treatment that the treatment is the thing. Why will a treatment do more good and become more effective at one time than another? It isn't because God listens; it isn't because we are better at one time than another. It is because there are times when we have a more complete acceptance of our own word than at another.

Therefore treatment is clarification of thought, it is clear thinking. I think it lets in more light than there was, more power, more love, more wisdom; opens a mystical doorway to a greater awareness when we treat; but it will still happen that the mechanics of it will be that the word is the thing. Now I believe this is the principal key to the whole thing. Once we admit a prayer can be answered or ever has been answered, we have admitted there is some kind of a something, whether it is God as a Parent, or Law Principle, or Presence—and I believe in the Principle and the Presence. We have admitted there is something that either acts upon our treatment or is acted upon by it in such a way that either the treatment is the thing, or the power operating upon the treatment becomes the thing—I don't know which any more than I know how an acorn becomes an oak tree. I don't know, nobody knows; it doesn't matter.

But let us suppose the treatment is the thing. I think the word I speak—"It is spirit and it is life," Jesus said; and I think he was right. Then our aim is not to speak the right word, necessarily, but *a* word that is so completely accepted that it can operate. And if its action is by reaction, and its response by correspondence, or by corresponding to our attitude toward it and in it, we must realize that there would be a mechanics and a mathematics, not in our giving the treatment, but in what happens when it is given. I believe the universe is a combination of spontaneous combustion and mathematical reaction—just another way of saying it is a divine Presence knowing, and a universal law responding at the level of the knowingness of the Presence.

We do not look upon God as a principle, but as a Presence. But I think the principle of the Law of Mind in Action is an action as mechanical as any other principle in the universe. It won't be a principle unless it is; it couldn't be. And it most certainly is a principle. Now there will then be some words. All words will have some power, some words will have more power, and some all power.

Jesus probably spoke words that had all power. He said, "Heaven and earth will pass away, but my words shall not till it is fulfilled." That was more than faith. It was more than conviction. I think to Jesus there was no difference saying that than for you and me to say the sun is shining. He didn't put any force into it; he didn't put any concentration into it; he didn't hold thoughts or will

141

anything to happen. He didn't suddenly get good and spiritual so God could give him a drink of water. Jesus was not superstitious; as a matter of fact the ones around him were, but he wasn't. He said, This is the way it is, and he likened the operation of that law, in his parables, to different laws of nature.

So some words will have more power than other words; some words theoretically would have all power; and all words would have some power. Now we look for the word that has all power, naturally. We should; and we would find that word. There is some conviction we have to surrender to our own word. I think that is what I am trying to say, and I hope it makes sense. I never thought of it that way before.

A conviction that we have, we will say we surrender to God—but isn't that surrendering it to the way you are doing it? And therefore we would have to have a conviction intellectually—and I think inwardly that what we are doing is true. I mean, it isn't make-believe. It isn't a sad, sweet song, it isn't a hymn of praise, it isn't a supplication. These things are not wrong, but it isn't these.

But it is a reality—and such a reality in our own mind that if we were treating for the disappearance of a stomach ulcer, it shouldn't be there when we get through treating. It should be dissolved. Now the only way we can prove it, and know this can be, is the proof of it. And the proof of it could take place while everybody was looking. I had just as soon a doctor would be attending a patient of mine, and giving them an examination every day if they wanted, as not; because that has nothing to do with "water being wet." If I conceded that it did, I would limit my treatment to the doctor's opinion and be a servant of the thing we obey. It is just another field of superstition.

As a matter of fact, probably the guy needs a doctor unless I can prove that he doesn't. I don't see any sense in knocking crutches out from under somebody; I think he should throw them away *if he doesn't need them.* Because we are controversial and contentious. However I think the real way is noncontroversial and noncontentious, along the theory that nonopposition is the only thing that cannot be opposed, nonresistance is the only thing that cannot be resisted, nonviolence is the only thing that cannot be violated. But we measure things from such a short distance that we don't realize that. We say Jesus was betrayed by his followers and he was crucified by the Romans and what was the sense of the love he had? Well, if a few hours of suffering is consequential in 2000 years of adoration, the balance is all in the favor of Jesus. It always is. Though the mills of God grind slowly, they grind exceeding small. Compensation is necessary, but Jesus knew and Gandhi knew and we all know to some degree, that there is no way to gain all without first giving all. There isn't any compromise, the Universe does not bargain with us. It doesn't say, If you are good I will send you sugar candy instead of a thunder bolt. There is no bargain we make with it; it has to be met on its own terms. But these terms are not arbitrary. God is Love.

We don't have to wonder if the Universe rests on the shoulders of Love when modern psychiatry sides with us. Did you see the notices recently of how the Lutherans have stopped preaching hell? If hell cooled off for the Lutherans, that would be something. And the Pope wants the Protestants to become Catholics—what a lack of a sense of wit! Evolution is forward, not backward.

The Universe has to meet us; we have to meet it on its terms. It is demonstrated that love is superior to hate. But, you know, we will never know *how* superior until everything is surrendered that is not lovely; that is our trouble. We would like to let go of it enough to squeeze through an almost closed gate; we still like to reserve the privilege of beating the hell out of a few others. But the Universe doesn't compromise with us.

It says, If you love, you have to love John Smith. He may be a stinker, but you have to love him. You have to love Mary Lou. She is a prostitute, but you have to love her. Because the Universe is that way. But we set up our little things.

If you want to get out of hell, then nobody can ever be in it. Why do you have it for one, who is just stewing in your own juice—? Nature, Emerson said, forevermore screens herself from the profane; but when the fruit is ripe it will fall. Nature never compromises with anything or anybody, or the exact laws of science, mathematical and mechanical and inexorable and immutable; but it is now believed even in physics that the old concept of cause and effect no longer holds good. This is very significant to a metaphysician because prior to Jesus they had believed that. The Jews, Mosaic law; the Hindus, the law of reincarnation and karma, which is the fruit of action—*karma* means the fruit of action. And so they taught the law of cause and effect—an eye for an eye, and a tooth for a tooth. You have to work out everything so you don't have to come back here in your karma.

Now Jesus did not contradict either one of these assumptions. He knew better ones. He knew of the instantaneous here and the eternal now. He knew of a Universe which had no history. And I have been thinking about that: God has no history, truth has no history. *We* have a history only because we consent to it. Who said, "History is a tale that is told"? Napoleon, that is right. And that is true. And Emerson said, "History is the record of the doings of that Mind on this planet."

The thing we are dealing with has no past and no future. It only has the present—but because our present is the past rehashed and our future is the present reenacted. That is a good idea. That is in accord with the whole law of karma and the law of cause and effect of Moses; and it is also in accord with the psychology of Freud in some ways, where he said a neurotic thought pattern will repeat itself with monotonous regularity throughout life.

I had one recently—a terrific neurosis—and I didn't like it very much, and it was of no consequence; they never are. My neurosis was attached to somebody, as it generally is. I thought one day, this is a very nice person that I am unconsciously displeased with (or whatever it may be). And I thought, this is a nice guy; I don't believe any of the things about him that I believe about him. So I got to thinking in retrospect and found that what I was believing about him was something that had happened to me several times throughout my life. And so I began to call him by the name of the places where it happened, sometimes 40 years ago; and the first thing I knew, the transference of the neurosis from this particular person was to the others, and from there to nothing—because it was ridiculous. Isn't that interesting?

This is true; this is a quick analysis. This is all that can happen to any analysis and is of no consequence. But I thought then, I wonder if all unhappiness, all impoverishment, all disease is not merely a neurotic thought pattern repeating itself over and over at our expense, and mostly from the experience of the whole human race—because I don't happen to believe that I am smart enough to have thought up all the good I have had or all the evil I thought I had; and I haven't had much evil. I don't think we are good enough to create a soul or bad enough to destroy it. It is here, and we are hell-bent for heaven; but we are mostly hell-bent too much of the time—and yet we are hell-bent *in* heaven, aren't we?

Some words will have all power, all words will have some power. The word that has all power must be a word to which we have surrendered everything that contradicts it. "Who has surrendered all hate to love; who has surrendered all unloveliness to love." Sidney Lanier* said that none of the singers ever yet has wholly lived his ministrelsy. Jesus said, if you want to know about this doctrine, try it. He knew darned well that anybody who did what he did would get the same results. Heaven has no pets.

God has no chosen disciples, the universe has no history; if it did, it would have ceased to exist before it started. It is difficult for us to conceive a timeless time in which a temporary time of necessity takes place so that the timeless shall express itself—an absolute absoluteness in which a relativity may transitorily transpire, in order that the absolute shall be expressed without the relativity ever being a thing in itself; and of course all the philosophers have known this. That is why St. Augustine said that time is attention, recollection, and then dissipation.

*American poet.

Dean Inge* said that time is a sequence of events in a unitary wholeness. I simplified it by saying that time is a measure of any experience, but it is never a thing in itself. It couldn't be, because there is something that compresses eternity into an hour and stretches an hour into eternity. But in our treatment then we would have to surrender everything. Now this is, I think, what Jesus meant by losing your life to find it. Jesus never lost his life or he wouldn't have been resurrected, because if he were dead, he would have been dead, period; and all the wailing of seven thousand angels would never have brought him to. He wasn't dead. This is a metaphor, an expression. We would have to give up unloveliness to be loved—there isn't any question; we would have to surrender all confusion to be at peace, and this isn't easy, because our neurotic thought patterns seem to operate on their own.

I believe it must be that everything that is a negation— everything that contradicts what ought to be and what has a right to be and what must be in Truth and in Reality—must, from the standpoint of that other thing, not be so. It couldn't be. Jesus said that the unreal never has been, the Real has never ceased to be; but the two are so confused. I am finding that the greatest difficulty in this thing that my brother and I are writing† is the section on Reality and Illusion. It has taken more of my time and thought than five other sections, and I haven't got it resolved yet, to put into print, because it is a very subtle thing: What is real and what isn't real.

Plotinus said that everything is as real as it is supposed

---

*William Ralph Inge, English prelate and author.
†*The Voice Celestial.* Ernest Holmes and Fenwicke Holmes (Los Angeles, Science of Mind Publications, 1960).

to be, but that nothing, or no thing, has any self-determination. All things, he said, are indeterminate. I like this much better than the assumption that *everything we don't like* is unreal, because I have watched the convolutions of the intelligences that exist in the brains of those who preach this doctrine, and I discover that finally this particular kind of absolutism runs around denying everything it doesn't like and affirming everything it does—and God is always on its side. It is a terrific psychological attitude to assume, but I couldn't quite take it. Plotinus said that everything is as real as it is supposed to be, but that nothing has self-determination. He said, "If I were to personify God, I would say I do not argue, I contemplate; and as I contemplate, I let fall the images of my thought, and they become things." As the Hermetic teaching said, Everything on earth is a copy of what is in heaven.

Now we would have to surrender: If we are treating for abundance, we have to surrender lack. This isn't easy, because someone says, "If I hurt, I hurt; and if I haven't got a dime, I know I haven't got a dime." But here is the cold Law. Someone says, "Well God wouldn't let it be that way." Well, that *is* the way it is; it isn't any other way. God did not say—of course God never said anything— that if you stand in front of a mirror you won't cast a reflection into it. We are bound to the reflection. It is the meaning of that famous story—would you call it an allegory?—of Plato's about the caves. He tells about the slaves, or these people who are in the caves, and they can't see out. All they see is their shadows, which seem to have chains, and they mistake the shadow for the substance. In other words, they are chained by the shadow of their own belief—but they *are* chained.

It would be impossible to speak a word of absolute prosperity and success while we believe in its opposite. How are we going to get around it? I suppose everybody coerces his own mind; I have to coerce mine—because you can't live in disagreement with yourself; it is psychically like trying to go two ways at once. But I do it this way: I have come to believe that the relative is the Absolute *as* the relative—very simple. Nothing has in itself or of itself to be denied—that there is absolutely no bondage as such, and that bondage is freedom—because in my system I cannot have any dualism. I never speak as an encyclical; this is just what *I* believe, and you don't have to believe it at all. Everybody has to get himself out of the doldrums, pull himself out of whatever trap he is in. I tried many years ago to arrive at it by denying everything that didn't seem good, and I found I was just denying everything I didn't like. I am not intelligent enough to pick the sheep from the goats.

So it is easier for me to say, I am bound by my own freedom, and my bondage is my freedom. But I don't like my freedom this way; therefore this thing hasn't anything to say about it. Then I remove a contention from my own mind. That helps me, because I think that in treatment there has to be flexibility. You are dealing only with yourself, and yet you have to be on pretty good terms with yourself to live. I think you have to believe in yourself. I don't think it is egotism to believe in yourself; I think it is a false assumption not to. But I believe in a self that I must get most of myself out of the way of. Can you get yourself out of the way long enough to know the truth about this? Because the truth is none of "your business." There is a truth that, known, is demonstrated; there is a word that is all power, even though all words have some power. *There would have to be a complete abandonment.*

Now I believe this is what faith has done throughout the ages. I don't care how they prayed; most people's God is grotesque, and probably ours is to a finer perception. We think we are way ahead of certain concepts, and I think we are, but there are probably concepts above ours since there are beings beyond us, as we are beyond a tadpole. I hold this as axiomatic. It has to be that way in a universe—not a universe that is expanding, but a universe in which all evolving things are expanding. Evolution is an effect and not a cause.

You never can explain anything if you put it as cause; but you can if you put it where it belongs: as an effect—as all the great have done. It is the very basis of Hindu philosophy—the divine spark that impregnates the mundane clod, containing in itself the essence of its own being and the pattern of its own performance, so that all evolution is merely the unfoldment of what was involuted. I believe in that. It is what the Bible speaks of as a pattern shown thee on the mount. It is an essential part of the Greek philosophy; but they got it through Pythagoras* via the Hermetic teaching. It came down originally from Egypt; a surprising amount of the Greek philosophy did, because Pythagoras went to Egypt and studied and traveled there.

So we would have to surrender. And I find it easier for me to say this thing—it is as real as it is supposed to be, but it hasn't any reality to itself, it is a shadow. Therefore I don't have to fight it, I don't have to argue against it; but here we have to have a complete surrender.

---

*Greek philosopher and mathematician.

Troward said it is not a surrender of a different kind of a power and essence; it is the surrender of the lesser to the greater, and it is only in degree—because the life of God is man; there is no other life. There is only one life. And I think this is what happened wherever prayer has been answered through faith; and plenty of it has, and so instantly that it is amazing—the most instantaneous cases of healing and manifestation the world has authentic records of. And the largest number do not come from the metaphysical field. Did you know that? They come from the field of orthodox prayer. I think we ought to gladly recognize it and intelligently analyze it; but they are very rare indeed, compared to the signs that follow the metaphysician, because he knows what he is doing.

But we must not overlook the fact that faith has produced these miraculous things, and instantly. Then we shall see that faith cooperated with the principle that we teach and believe in (though we don't always have the conviction); there is a sort of emotionalism that went with it. But very few people ever had it compared to the people in our field who work it out more or less axiomatically and mechanically and grind it out by hand—it is better, and something you can teach people: that the intellect and emotions surrendered; and the will, in a moment of exaltation, got enough clearance in the mind to let something happen before the subconscious reaction set in.

I remember being in New York many years ago when a Dr. Hixson was there, a healer in the Episcopal church by the laying on of hands. A man came to me and said he had a very prominent goiter and that the doctor had healed it. Then, he said, he went away and the goiter came back. Then Dr. Hixson healed it again and it went away; and then came back again. This is a very interesting thing to one who thinks: the fervor of the prayer, the conviction, the faith of a very wonderful man dissolved a form—but the image was still there, and it restored the form. But I am interested in the fact that it dissolved the form. We will say that it melted some ice but didn't change the temperature of the atmosphere, so the water froze again.

But it does give proof of the liquidity of the water, and, in that higher temperature, of the nonsolidity of that which denied the liquidity. I am talking about ice and water of course. The goiter disappeared—it made two grand disappearances and two grand reappearances, like most of our prima donnas. It finally went away and didn't come back. Here was the subjective image of the seed of the thing.

What constitutes a science of Mind is that we know these things, and we know that there is a cumulative power in treatment. It *is* cumulative. We know that it is cumulative in its effectiveness. What I am trying to say is, it will be a direct-ratio proportion mathematically and mechanically to the inward acceptance of the word. The objective manifestation will have nothing to do with it. It hasn't anything more to do with it than a piece of ice can say "I won't melt" when it is in the sun. It has nothing to say about it. The only question is, does the ice get in the sun? But we limit it, you see; and when we limit it, we change the atmosphere. We say "Maybe; maybe —maybe I don't know enough; maybe I am not good enough; maybe this person resists, maybe I can't help this person because he doesn't believe I can."

All of this has nothing to do with it whatsoever, if our

theory is correct. It only takes one person to know. And having realized that this can happen, then we have to know that it only takes one person to know. It wouldn't take a thousand. A thousand persons knowing something wouldn't make it more or less true than one person knowing it would. The truth known would have to demonstrate itself. Mrs. Eddy said that truth known is demonstrated. Jesus said, "Ye shall know the truth and the truth shall make you free."

Now we have to feel the absolute independence of what we are doing, the absolute authority of what we are doing. I don't believe words have much power unless there is authority in them. I think the authority is not an assumption, and I don't think the authority is merely an affirmation or a vehement proclamation. It is the authority of the knowledge of the way that it has to be; it is the authority of somebody who said, "I will plant this seed, and it will produce a plant." This is absolute authority.

It is the same authority as if I should say, "This is a watch." If I were to spend the rest of my life thinking up an affirmation that I do not myself deny, I couldn't think one up any more complete than to say, "This is a watch." When I say, "This is a watch," there is nothing in me to say, "Maybe it is a clock." There isn't anything in me to say, "Is it really a watch?" or to ask any other question about it. It is just a watch, and neither God nor man can make a more powerful statement. But it is simple, isn't it?

Nothing in me doubts it; I know it is a watch. I wouldn't say their or anybody's thought can influence whether this is a watch, let all the world deny it and the ages deny it. Jesus said, "Stretch forth your hand." He didn't argue with what people believe; he didn't care who believed the man was born blind because his grandfather had done something to someone. This was twaddle to him. Isn't it strange that the most powerful thing we can say or think has no psychological forced positiveness about it.

We are redeemed from fear and superstition; I just haven't got any. Therefore we are not afraid to make the assumption of authority lest something blast us. In other words, we are not afraid of the Universe in which we live. We know the Universe has no history; it can't have. God is not growing up—that is a cinch to me. We know that there could be nothing to contradict whatever the truth is; there is not the truth and something else. This we know. There is not something plus nothing, leaving nothing equal to something. We know there must be a word that has all power. Now we must know that we can speak it, and listen to it.

So let's do it, and let's know we do surrender everything that is unreal, everything that says "it can't," or "you hadn't ought to," "you are not good enough to," "you don't know enough." We surrender everything that denies the divine Presence, the divine Reality, the universal Law of Good, the love, the fatherhood, the brotherhood, the Unity. This Unity necessitates fatherhood and brotherhood and motherhood and sonship—you and I haven't anything to do with it, but we enter into the joy of that inheritance, into the limitless calm of that universal peace, into the bliss of that eternal Light which casts no shadow; we are alive, conscious, awake. This is not the surrender of action or movement or purpose or intention, or accomplishment or the drama or joy of life, or the song of life. It is quite the reverse.

All these things exist that the one singer shall sing in us. Therefore we surrender everything that denies the song which is beyond all songs, which we sing. All of the love there is in the Universe is right here, in our experience now, right now—it is not by and by—all of the abundance, all of the glory, all the good, all the peace, all the power, all the joy and all the gratification.

Now we know that everything we do shall be prospered, made happy—no waiting, no procrastination, no deferment, no delay. This word is what we are doing; what we are doing is this word. They are inseparable. This word is the law and the thing and everything. And now we know that everything we touch shall be blessed—everything. There is nothing can go from us to any person but a blessing; nothing but life, nothing but joy, nothing but happiness. There is no morbidity, no hurt, no fear, no lack, no want, no limitation. We shall bless and heal everything we touch without even being aware of it, just like a light is light—"So let your light shine"—and we believe in that light; it is real. So everything is made whole, everything is healed that needs healing, everything is made glad and happy and bursts into a song, everything is prospered. This is the law of our lives. We will it so, we decree it so, we announce it, we surrender everything that denies it. And having isolated and surrendered everything that denies it, there is nothing left but the central fact that affirms it—that we are That. So it is.

CHAPTER 10

What Is Spiritual Mind Healing?

N O MATTER HOW OFTEN they are told, many people do not understand the significance of spiritual mind healing nor what it is nor what it is based on. Most people think we are materializing spirit or spiritualizing matter or that we are influencing lower planes by a higher plane—and there is no such thing—or that we have suddenly gotten so spiritual that God sits up and takes notice. There is no such God, and there are no such people. I wish there were such people but know there couldn't be such a God.

I was trying to explain to a man last night that the universe as such—that the manifest universe—must exist, as Aurobindo said, for the delight of God, and that the universe as such has no purpose as theology teaches purpose. The only purpose an infinite and unobstructed Being could have would be to express Itself as what It knows Itself to be. It hasn't the purpose of saving Its own creation, because It doesn't know that Its creation is lost.

We were discussing the possibility of some great metaphysical play, something that would contain the affirmative factors, and he was telling me how difficult it is when the producer gets ready to make a picture. He said that by the time they have taken it to the Catholics and then to the Jews and then to the Protestants and they are all pleased, the "hell" is beat out of it and there is nothing left but a little sweet love story that doesn't mean anything or do anything, and he said that very few people realize what a terrible handicap this is in producing real pictures.

If we produce a religious picture the way we think about it, somebody else might not believe in it. It would be a wonderful thing if such a picture could be made. So few people understand the basis for our treatment; so few people understand what is meant if we say that we are living in a spiritual universe governed by mental law and that all substance itself, whether it is formed or formless, is merely mind in action—or, as Quimby said, matter is mind in form and mind is matter in solution—that the treatment is not a mental or spiritual thing, operating upon a physical or material something; that the apparent material and physical something is not any different from the formless part of itself—it is merely the form that that same substance takes, because thought could not affect anything other than that which was a product of mind, could it?

Whether we say with Mrs. Eddy that all is infinite Mind in manifestation, which is a pretty good way of saying it—except if she were living today, she would not be talking about a material universe, because there isn't any; nobody believes in any; science doesn't believe in a material universe as they thought of it 75 years ago—or whether we say with Spinoza,* "I don't say mind is one

*Benedict de Spinoza, Dutch philosopher (1632-1677).

thing and matter is another, but I say they are the same thing." Or whether we say with Quimby, "Mind is matter in solution, and matter is mind in form." Or whether we say with the Bible that the invisible things of God from the foundation of the world are manifest by the visible. It doesn't make any difference.

We are really saying—or, with Einstein—energy and mass are equal, identical, and interchangeable. They are all saying that what you see and what you do not see is the same thing, except what you do not see is what you do see when you can see it. But here is the whole basis of spiritual mind treatment consciously used or scientifically used or applied definitely for a specific purpose, and this is why people who originated these ideas, like Quimby, Mrs. Eddy, and others—no one person; *all* of them—had insisted that treatment is not faith healing.

This is no denial of the benefits of faith healing, because faith healing would undoubtedly utilize the principle which may be consciously used. We believe and know that a definite statement made in mind produces a specific result in a neutral field, or, as Kimball* said, this treatment or this argument logically presented to mind produces a certain result. Quimby said, "I stand as a lawyer stands to his client"; and he said, "I enter the man of opinions, so to speak, and I represent the man of wisdom, and I explain that what is wrong are his opinions manifest, because matter is mind in form and mind is matter in solution." Then he said that the thing will work like mathematics. That is where we got the idea of mathematical conclusions; it came from Quimby entirely, at least as an original concept.

*Edward A. Kimball, celebrated teacher of Christian Science.

And he said, "You ask what the cure is, and my answer is that my explanation is the cure." All he meant by that was, if his explanation contains an evidence in its wording that is accepted, it will produce a result. Then the other fellow [Kimball] said, this argument logically presented to mind produced this result. Now this is very interesting, because 75 to 90 percent of all healing that has ever been done in the metaphysical field has been done by a process of argument, of affirmation and denial, followed by as much realization as the person has at that time. Because no matter how much they all contradict each other in the New Thought field, they all, when it comes to practice, do the same thing exactly. And since something happens, we have to assume that there is a medium through which it happens—which is exactly like what Troward called the Universal Subjectivity.

But here again there is a very great confusion over that, because when we speak of a Universal Subjectivity and an individual subjective, we are liable to be misled into the assumption that there is an individual mind and an individual law, which isn't true at all. We are very liable to believe that the Universal Subjectivity, as people call it (or as he called it), is a thing in itself—which it never is.

Everything that bears the mark of subjectivity, the subconscious, the unconscious—the subconscious and unconscious of psychology and the subjectivity of the psychic and metaphysical field—is never a thing in itself. Is that clear? It may look like it, it may act it, it may repeat itself with monotonous regularity, it may control the destiny of the race—which I guess it does—but it is never a thing in itself. It is always an effect operating in a medium which acts as though what is believed in is true.

But it is always subject to a greater truth, or to *the*

Truth. Plotinus referred to it as a blind force—not knowing, only doing. Now as Troward said, this medium, whether we call it our own subjective which has no existence, or a Universal Subjectivity which exists as law but not as person—not as something which can be aware of what it is doing or how to do it—acts without even knowing that it is acting or why. Would that be clear?

People mistake the concept of law with the idea of God —and the idea of God is no more the concept of mental law than the idea of God is the concept of electricity or gravitational force. There is so much superstition about it all, very little clarity of thought; because the Law will always remain, as Troward said, impersonal, plastic, neutral—but creative and intelligent, having no mind of its own. Plotinus said the same thing. It and all creation, he said, are indeterminate; not illusion—they are not unreal; they are as real as they are supposed to be—but they are not self-determinate. They exist there as an effect.

Now spiritual mind treatment consciously used, then, is a definite and persistent and consistent attempt to think straight and logically, basing the assumption on a concept of an undivided and indivisible spiritual Universe here and now, and translating everything into the terms of Mind in action as law, and conscious intelligence as directive power. There isn't a branch of metaphysics that would escape coming under these two categories of Presence and Person, and Law and Order.

Now the Law and Order themselves are merely the way the Presence and Person manifest. They are the way. It is a very interesting thing, because no matter what science we may be studying or looking into—all scientific investigation, physics and everything else—we don't deny anything it teaches. We believe it is true if it is true: What is true is true. We just affirm this, however—and I am sure they would too—that all science watches the operation of the Law and the way it works and what it does; not what it is or why. Science cannot answer *what* nor *why*—only *how*—in the operation, and doesn't pretend to. Neither can we.

Now why would that be? Because there is no God who could explain to Himself, or to anything else, what God is. There is no God who could justify His own being by explanation, because that which can explain is not First Cause; it is secondary cause explaining its relationship to Primary Cause. Therefore there is no God to argue with, and no God who knows anything about an argument, and no God who argues.

Now we have to assume as the basis of everything— the whole basis—that there is such a self-existent principle of Mind and such a self-existent awareness, Presence, or consciousness as a Supreme Being or as God or as the Spirit, and that they are inexplicable; that the Law knows nothing but to do, and the Presence knows of nothing that can contradict It.

The history of the whole human race is in the operation of the Law. Whether it is true or false doesn't matter; this is where the ancients got the idea of the illusion of mind and the illusion of matter, or form, because they knew one was as great an illusion as the other. Whether or not they had our concept of their being the same thing I don't know. Sometimes I think they did, and sometimes I am not sure, but it doesn't matter; *we* do. But we have to see that in the operation of what Mrs. Eddy called the mortal mind, and the Bible called the carnal mind, and Troward called race suggestion, and Jung called the collective unconscious, we see not the operation of an entity

161

in Mind but the operation of a Mind principle responding to what was, and may still be, an entity individually or collectively—and endlessly repeating the errors of the ages. And individualizing them until some individual consciously or unconsciously individualizes himself out of the law of averages that is established throughout the ages by the consensus of human opinion and experience. Does this make it any clearer?

If somebody believes that a certain planet affects him, then what everybody who ever lived thought about the effect of that planet will now affect him. But the planet itself won't be affecting him; it will be the belief about the effect of the planet. And because it will work like mathematics, everybody will say it must be true—because it does work like mathematics. Everything works like mathematics; everything in operation is operating in a field of mathematics and mechanics. And everything has color and tone, I think—definitely. And everything looks as though it were depending upon itself—and there is nothing seen or in operation that could depend upon itself. Otherwise the only creator that there would be would be a blind force. And the very fact that we can differentiate between heat and cold, the very fact that we can affirm or deny anything, shows that the primary cause is not a blind force. The very fact that I could deny God is proof that there is no God who could be affected by my denial.

It is the very proof of the possibility of more than one kind of experience even in the field of unitary wholeness, or what the Ancient Hindus called the period of ignorance and our theology more crudely calls sin. You know, the Christian theology is much more crude than the Hindu philosophy; but don't say I said so. It isn't as well thought out. Salvation by grace only is not as well thought out as salvation by works; but we have to combine both of them.

The period of ignorance—now this is the background of what is called Eden. In theology we have sin and salvation. And the story of the Garden of Eden is a story, and it just didn't happen this way, that is all. But here is a story to adorn a principle. Every religion has told it, and all in the world they mean is this: Whether it were planned or not—and we don't believe in divine plan—the creative principle operates in such a way that it automatically and arbitrarily supplies the evolving instrumentality with everything necessary to complete its journey. Browning called it a spark that disturbs our clod. It is called the Atman in Hinduism; it is Christ in our religion; it is an Avatar; it is a Buddha—all it means is this: it is the incarnation of the Divine in the mundane, and it is referred to in our Bible as Satan falling like a flame of fire or something, and landing on the earth, and theology interpreted it as their having had a terrible fight up there and having thrown the guy overboard—very crude theology; not very much finesse to it.

But it means the impregnation of the mundane clod by the divine spark of life—what Troward refers to in the first chapter of *Bible Mystery, Bible Meaning*, as the period of involution which precedes evolution. Involution is a spontaneous thing, and evolution is a mathematical outworking of it, whether it takes what you and I measure as a year or what we might measure as millennium, and it is what the Old Testament in Genesis refers to as the generation of the time when the plant was in the seed before the seed was in the ground. In other words, the divine idea before it was embodied by a process of law and action and reaction was entirely spontaneous, and every seed contained it. All the poets have referred to it in one way or another; it is the foundation of all teaching of the beginning of the individuation of the Spirit. But of a necessity if this is going to produce that which will sometime—let us say in a very human way—return to it that which was given, it has to set it in motion and let it alone.

There is no such thing as mechanical spontaneity. There is a mechanics in the universe, but it is a reactive thing to that which is spontaneous, self-explosive, self-assertive, whose law operates mechanically and mathematically but itself is neither mechanics nor mathematics but is a spontaneous self-proclamation. That is why one of the oldest sayings in the world is, "Spirit is the power that knows itself." We believe absolutely in the God who is Self-Knowing, but not self-knowing as though a God said, "Here I am, but there you are over there"—but the God who knows and whose self-knowing is in us at the level of our self-knowing; and that level of our self-knowing is Its knowing in us at that level. Therefore we believe that the relative is the Absolute at the point of the relative. It is not an illusion at all. Therefore you don't have to get all messed up in higher mathematics or higher metaphysics by finally coming to the place where you have a great reality and a great illusion. There is no such thing.

Plotinus, whom Inge called the King of Intellectual Mystics of the Ages, said that everything is as real as it is supposed to be, but nothing has self-determination. Quimby said that all things are really liquid, taking enough form to express themselves; but they are really liquid, and there is no difference between the mind that formed them and the form that is what they are. And common sense will teach us that if that were not true, a thought could not dissolve a form, could it? If the form were separate from thought, if it were something different from the nature of mind, then they couldn't get together at all. Impossible.

But let's get back to this idea; it interests me very much, because Aurobindo speaks of it as the period of ignorance —the Christians call it the Fall, the sin, and salvation. Emerson—who saw beyond Christianity, because he said that we have confused Jesus with virtue in the possibility of all men; and that is quite a slice of reason—of course was familiar with all of the old teachings; that the only way individuation can spring full-orbed is to start out with the potential. Browning said, "a God though in the germ." So if there are, as I believe, beings beyond us as we are beyond a tadpole, and then beyond that: in the sequence of that evolution of being there will never be a moment that we don't know ourselves and belong to the plane on which we live; and it won't be any different than it is here, in a sense—but *more*. There won't be a loss of what we are, but always more added to it. We would have to be let alone to discover ourselves, while the compulsory and mechanical necessities of evolution, or laws, would work automatically, just as the automatic working of certain parts of our physical body has nothing to do with our thought—like the genes that, Williams says, in the fruit of the family tree are never affected by anyone but are brought to each generation in the Ark of the Covenant of God. Isn't that interesting?

Otherwise we would have destroyed all creation. If any individual or group of individuals have the power they would like to have, God help the rest of us. I am a great believer that when the fruit is ripe, it will fall; but as

Emerson said, "Nature forever more screens herself from the profane." No great amount of spiritual power, in my estimation, is delivered to anyone—and I don't mean a God that withholds it and delivers it; but one just can't take it until one takes it in its own nature, and its own nature is Unity and Goodness and Truth and Beauty and Reason. Not that there is a God who withholds it; but we can't take it till we can reach it, let's say.

At any rate, we would account for the endless ages of stupidity and trouble because of ignorance; and yet we would see that this is the only way we should ever spring full-orbed into being, and we would see another thing: that God and nature, the Universe, withholds nothing from anyone—it is all delivered. This is what I interpret as the Christian theology of grace. Not grace because Jesus was a nice guy; that is weakness. Grace because the Universe is Itself an infinite givingness—It can't help it; that is Its nature—and because it is in our own experience only the one who gives all who gets all. There isn't any other perscription—that is it. As you give, you get—good measure pressed down and running over; the eternal circuits—because there is a justice without a judgment, and that justice is merely the balance and equilibrium of the Universe. It has to be there, and we suffer not because of the judgment imposed upon us but because of the judgment of ignorance. That is why Emerson said there is no sin but ignorance and no salvation but enlightenment.

Now just as every other law awaits our recognition of it, it doesn't know it is waiting. The law back of our ability to have television didn't know it was waiting until somebody discovered how to use it; it was just there, and when somebody used it, it didn't *appear*, but it *went into operation*, because that is the way it works. It doesn't seem strange to me that the time should come in the evolution of the human race when some people like we are—for this is what I think is the part we play in evolution, as well as all people who believe as we do; millions of them in the world—should come to see that spiritual law is natural law, that the Universe in which we live is a spiritual system and makes sense, that ignorance of the law excuses no one from its effect, as people say. If these things are true, why doesn't the Bible tell you so? The Bible does not give you a recipe for pancakes, much less this type of thing. Something new is emerging in the world. This is not an old philosophy warmed over, nor even the Christian faith with a little something added and warmed up. This is itself, according to the eternal verities of the Universe, taking place at all times and as entirely new things appear which were not preceded by logical parentage; and every science recognizes it—biology and horticulture and everything.

There is a principle back of all evolution which responds to the demand made upon it in the terms of the demand, good, bad, or indifferent; right or wrong as we understand it—this principle doesn't know anything about any of this. It just acts by reacting, and reacts by correspondence, exactly like a mirror; but there is infinite intelligence back of it. And so we find—someone must have understood this—"As in Adam all die, in Christ all are made alive." The original of that is, As in the first Adam we all die, so in the second Adam—which is Adam Cadmon—we all live. The second Adam is Christ, Buddha, or Atman—the same thing. All it means is that limitation dies.

I asked Adela* yesterday to write a story about the principle of the Resurrection—not necessarily the Resurrection of Jesus; just to suggest it and to say that for every death there must be a resurrection, and for every resurrection there had to have been a death of something—if it were only that you are less mean today than you were yesterday. The more mean had to die to get the less mean resurrected, didn't it? It is a principle of transcendence, forever flowing in where we let go; "nought is the squire when the King's at hand; withdraw the stars when dawns the sun's brave light"—or as somebody said, the full gods will have to come when the half gods go. But we should look back to that principle operating where whenever a demand is made upon it, it will answer in the terms of the demand made. And now some group of people have come to realize this and will perceive the meaning of the mystic who says, "Act as though I am and I will be." Jesus said it too: Believe and it will be done. And since there is now a spontaneous reaction to a mechanical actor, as far as you and I are concerned we might get a great wallop out of it or a little kick, just in experimental work. Everything isn't cut and dried and done.

I think we are laboring and belaboring and belabored and fussing, like climbing a tough hill where every time we take two steps we fall back one and half; because we are still climbing a hill. And the hill will be there as long as we see it. That is why Mrs. Hopkins said there is a group of people—she is referring to Old Testament people—who while they believed that God was all there was and had an exalted idea of God, always saw themselves

*Adela Rogers St. Johns.

as oppressed and in the valley of dry bones having attached to a race something that doesn't belong to it. We all have done it.

But as we try to conceive that there is no otherness, there is no difference, there is no opposition—that everything that is an effect is a sequence of a cause set in motion without knowing why—we would see that ignorance is the only sin there is. We should see that no one could measure the possibility of thought, no one could say it cannot be that way; no one has ever yet disproved what I am saying—no one—by logic, reason, or experimentation—no one ever will. Insofar as anyone has tried either to prove or disprove it, they have proven it. Therefore we have every justification in the world of trying to arrive at that transcendent state of consciousness where there is no argument and no contention, no opposition and no otherness, and where our own nonresistance will dissolve everything that seems to be resistant, because nothing can resist nonresistance. Nothing—just nothing.

Two icebergs will destroy battleships, because on this level force meets with equal force—and that is a law too. But the iceberg cannot resist the heat of the sun. This is why Aurobindo said that transcendence does not reconcile, it transmutes. Isn't that interesting? Jesus said, resist not evil and it will flee from you. Gandhi taught nonviolence. And they were both right.

Now there is nothing below the level of a certain thought. (I am not talking about good sweet thoughts.) It is like all the great questions that great people have asked, announcements they have made: something in us says, Yes; and we spend the rest of our time until we know what it is. There would be at any particular level of thought (everything that is below it is subservient to it) *everything*; not *something*. It doesn't matter who believed what or how many believed which.

I was interested in something someone said last night about some very prominent Catholic woman saying, "What right does this man have to say there is no hell and that there is nothing to be afraid of? Well," she said, "we are saved from hell only by fear." We are so afraid of the Universe that we are not sure but what God will knock our teeth out if we do say "hell." We worship the devil and are afraid of evil and are bound by a rope of sand in our whole belief about limitation. I think the most logical thing in the world for Jesus to do was to tell Lazarus to get up; and if Lazarus hadn't come out, Jesus would have crawled in.

I don't think it was strange he turned the water into wine. That is what they happened to want. There is a slow process in nature that does this; but who shall say it has to be done that way, beyond the time when somebody knows it doesn't have to be done that way—? Ignorance of the law excuses no one from its effect. Who shall say but what the very law that tramples the grapes of wrath will produce a celestial wine? And because it is too good to be true, and because it is so completely opposite to what we have believed, people will say they speak with a certain madness. They said Jesus was crazy, you know.

We are dealing with this kind of a transcendence and we may as well know it, because expectancy speeds progress—and if we don't have a conviction that "it can be," we are going to have a conviction that "probably it can't." Just as I have often said to you—and I told this fellow last night; he said it is an idea for his play—when Jesus fed the multitude, in all this throng the only person who could help him was the kid that didn't know it couldn't be done. The rest knew it couldn't be done, and why. He didn't know it couldn't be done. Jesus knew it could be done.

I always liken it in my own thought to that spontaneous thing, that child in us that never dies. We ought to carry him right along into our experience and if we think we have any wisdom—because all of our wisdom and all of our experience *he knew* before we got there. All of it. It is what Wordsworth refers to in the "Ode on Immortality" when he says that the youth is nature's priest. But, he said, "Ever more the prison walls' experience clothes him round," until finally he forgets that "celestial palace whence he came." But he further said, "In moments of calm weather though inland far we be,/ Our souls still have sight of that immortal sea/ That brought us hither, can in a moment transport us thither,/ And see the children sport upon the shore/ And hear the mighty billows rolling ever more."

As metaphysicians, then, instead of crashing round the icebergs and beating them against one another—which I think we do a lot, and everything kind of shatters—we ought to be more like the sun that shines nonresistantly, but remember: persistently. It isn't a weakness that it doesn't assert itself and scream how hot it is. It is a state of being; and we have to do that. So let's do it.

Let's treat our Santa Monica group—I want that place packed Sunday. And we know to here come the just and good and wise and those who can receive our message in joy and happiness, in recognition and with resolve to use it; and we know they are blessed by being there, and everyone who is there is healed. It is a transcendent experience for all of us. Whoever can be helped and healed is drawn there because you are saying it.

And we know we are establishing the law of our own being right here, the law of our life, that everything we touch is healed. There is a transcendence in us, there is the originating power and force and will and consciousness, the know-how. No matter what we call it, it is God, it is the real self too. Now this is the Son: nonresistant, nonargumentative, noncritical, noncondemning—this Thing which dwells forever more in the secret place within, healing and making everything whole It touches. It is our will, our desire, our acceptance that everything we touch shall spring into joy and happiness and laughter and truth and beauty.

Now let's do another thing: let's know we have great joy in life; that all heaviness and burden—the weight—falls away, as this spontaneous Thing springs into its own Self-Existence and the light of Its own truth and the love of Its own givingness, the power of its own Self-Existence. Let's see if we cannot know that without any conscious effort everything we touch is healed—every person, every situation—and that without any effort this perception continues to be with us. Now we know that there is no law of the past that limits, no belief of human mind whether we call it stars or whatever we call it—there is nothing that operates but the Truth, nor can nor ever will, and we embrace the Universe and everything in it and love it. It is beautiful, and we are perfect beings living in a perfect Universe surrounded by perfect beings and perfect situations—and we shall admit nothing else. Therefore we do not have to clash on the level of resistance.

CHAPTER 11

Basic Treatment Work

[Ernest read his poem of the Fable and some parts of "Illusion"]

EVERY RELIGION THAT ever existed has taught the main ideas contained in this, and this is just the way I said it. Our Bible says, "A mist went up from the face of the earth," etc. I wanted to get your reaction because there has to be a background for this whole section on Reality and Illusion,* what is real and what isn't, without making anything absolutely unreal. I do not believe in the unreality of anything, other than the illusion of our perspective of the thing, which must have some reality, else it wouldn't be there.

Plotinus, whom Inge called the king of intellectual mystics, said everything is as real as it is supposed to be, but things in themselves have no self-determination—they are indeterminate; and I think our philosophy is very close to that. Aurobindo is very emphatic and denies much of the theory of Buddhism, which he thinks is a theory of nihilism. I was reading something of his last night where

*Ch. 7 of First Book of *The Voice Celestial*, by Ernest and Fenwicke Holmes.

he said, in the true perspective matter is the complement of spirit and necessary to it, and is not unreal at all—and I believe this. God's world is not a world of illusion.

Bill* and I are doing questions and answers on the radio, and one last night I believe was truly an inspiration. I don't know what the questions are till he asks them, and this was about two different religious beliefs—Should a Catholic and Protestant marry?—and I got something of an inspiration and said, "If people view it rightly, each would feel there is a contribution of the other and both would come to greater fulfillment from the two different heritages." And this would be right if we weren't so little in our own consciousness.

Our concept is that we live in a spiritual universe right now. God is not evolving—nothing has happened to God; but within this Thing which does not evolve, there is a continual manifestation of life and an evolution of forms, ad infinitum, forever—never more but always less; but all motion takes place within That which does not move. That has been the teaching of the Ages. It does not make movement an illusion, but it backs it up at every point by the substantiality of That which does not have to move—and this is why Lao-tzu said, "All things are possible to him who can perfectly practice inaction." That sounds silly, but it isn't. Our Bible says, "Be still and know that I am God"—because it is out of the Silence that all movement comes. It is within the Silence that all movement takes place; and it is out of the Unmanifest that manifestation comes; and the first basic principle we

---

*William H. D. Hornaday, Religious Science minister and close associate of Ernest Holmes.

have to suppose is that creation, the act of creation, is merely the act of a creative Principle operating upon Itself, and out of Itself making what It creates—and what It creates is still Itself as the Creation.

The creation is not an illusion; people *do* have livers and lungs, etc. There is no illusion anywhere, and everything put in place will belong "to all the parts of one stupendous whole,/ Whose body nature is with God the soul." And our poet said, "Nothing useless is or low,/ Each thing in its place is best;/ And what seemed but idle show/ Strengthens and supports the rest."

We believe—or I believe—in everything. The child at play is not an illusion; but there is more playing than the child. I was talking to a man the other night about creating an atmosphere in a scene—he never heard of me and probably will never hear of me, but he happened to come in where we were and sat there for while—and he said, "I am more relaxed than I have been in six months; what goes on?" he said; "it has something to do with you." I said, "I am just a relaxed screwball," and he said, "Whatever it is . . . "and we got to talking, and I said, "This may sound screwy to you," and I talked good metaphysics applied to his profession. And he said, "I have known this all my life!" Isn't that interesting! He would make the most wonderful metaphysician, because his business is in making the illusive real, in making the soundless things speak, in making the silence speak, in making the unknown normal, in creating an atmosphere which everybody feels—and I understand he is one of the best in his field.

Now we don't believe anything out here is an illusion —but we don't believe anything out here makes itself; and

175

the thing that differentiates our philosophy from all others—I don't mean only Religious Science; I mean all metaphysicians, Unity, Christian Science, Divine Science, etc.; I am talking about the modern metaphysical movement as a whole—there is a philosophy they have and teach and practice that is not understood by any other group of people living, or whoever lived; and don't ever think something new hasn't come into the world with Quimby, Mrs. Eddy, and the New Thought leaders of early times—a new philosophic thing was announced, a basis and a new practicality; because contrary to what most people believe, we do not influence anything or anybody, we do not suggest anything to anyone or anything, we do not spiritualize matter and we do not materialize spirit. And we are not using good with which to combat evil or righteousness to overcome unrighteousness or good to overcome evil or God to beat the devil over the head with a cosmic club—this is exactly what we do NOT do.

Our whole practice and theory is based on the assumption that the visible and the invisible are just as Einstein said about energy and mass: equal, identical, and interchangeable. Spinoza had said the same thing, only he said, "I don't say mind is one thing and matter is another." And when Quimby said, "Mind is matter in solution and matter is mind in form," and Mrs. Eddy said, "All is infinite Mind and its infinite manifestation," they were all saying the same thing—and the Bible says, "The invisible things of God are made known by the visible," etc.

Now it is only on the assumption that nothing moves but Intelligence that we can give a treatment. Eddington said that we can think of all the laws of nature as though they were intelligence acting as law, and Jeans* said that we can think of it as an infinite thinker thinking mathematically. We believe that while the thought is spontaneous, the way it works and what happens is a mathematical and mechanical reaction. Pythagoras saw this; he said that all is motion and number, but there is a Mover. Music can be reduced to numbers too, I believe. So can the whole universe. But remember this: you have not explained the operation of the universe when you say it can be reduced to mathematics, because mathematics does not know that mathematics is mathematics. You see, if we stopped there, we would have nothing; so this is a fallacy. The engine can be known only because there is an engineer. That is why our two great assumptions are Presence and Person, and Law and Order. And that has been held throughout the ages.

Now our whole method of technique and practice proceeds on the assumption and basis and theory that Law is Mind in action, and that wherever we create a mental state relative to anything, and identify that thing with it, that which we recognize in our statements, realize and speak into them, tends to become true as to this situation; and because it does, whatever we put into the treatment will come out of it. Say, "This is the law of elimination to whatever is discordant, whatever doesn't belong; this establishes harmony"—it will do it.

Now the next thing is *why* and *how*. Nobody knows. Don't ever try to explain the why or the how, but only the way it works. Science can watch a process of the birth

---

*Sir James Jeans, English physicist.

of anything and say that at this stage this happens, and at that stage that happens; until finally they will have it worked out as a principle. Each day of incubation something happens to produce the chicken. But how it can happen they can't answer, or why it can happen they don't try to answer—only *the way through which* the how and the why operate to produce the what, which itself alone knows.

Someone was talking to me this morning about a case, where there are several different attitudes, in settlement of something. We don't give advice; I don't have any advice to give or know what to do. But I do say that there is something that does know; and when I say that there is something that knows relative to this action, I do not create the something that knows, but I do set the stage for that which knows to now know this. According to the theory of all emergent evolution, whenever a demand is made upon the principle, it answers in the terms of the demand made. What I mean is like this:

Say you are inventing something: when you announce this thing, the creative principle, acting as law, accepts the answer and intuitively and instinctively and innately knows—without knowing that it knows—what the answer is and produces it. Now I am not talking about God the Spirit; I am talking about the Universe of Law and Order. If that were not true, Luther Burbank could not have done the things he did. He made a demand on the intelligent creativity of the soil. Neither the soil, the potato or tomato, or Luther knew what would happen—and this principle didn't know consciously what would happen and doesn't know now. But it will always have to happen, because certain combinations will produce inevitable results. That is what I mean by saying that the principle acts by reacting: it reacts to the demand made upon it by answering that demand. This is held even in academic circles—in the departments of philosophy; what they call emergent evolution.

This is why Jesus said, "The words that I speak, they are spirit and they are life." There wasn't any question in the mind of Jesus but what his word was going to become a thing in this Law, and do exactly what he implied in his own consciousness it would do: "Go, thy servant is healed"; "Turn water from one jug into another and it will be wine"; "Cast your net over here"; etc., etc. Jesus was not like some man who would go into a grocery story and want stringbeans and ask for succotash. He was the most direct, most specific person who ever lived—at least one of them. And so we are dealing with a principle which not only receives the impress of our thought and acts upon it creatively; it is a principle which knows within itself what to do. So if we say, "I want a machine that will blow holes in spaghetti," this thing will think up such a machine. It just responds by announcement.

So I said, "I don't know anything about these legal matters; but I know this: right here, there is justice; truth; no lie; no liar; no one to tell a lie or believe one; no misrepresentation." And I said to this person, "I am not treating for you to win a case. I wouldn't do that. But truth and justice will prevail. Nobody can be lied to. What more do we want than the absolute truth?" I wouldn't treat in a controversy like this for anyone; I always ask if they think I am treating for them to win a point of law.

How do I know but what they are the liar? And they always say, "Oh no—it is right."

What is the principle involved here? The principle that enables us to treat from One Principle and One Substance, just because it is the unitary cause of everything—to treat for anything or all things that come out of the One Thing; and if it is necessary to have a specific something, then we will get it.

Now the whole principle and practice and possibility of the answer to prayer is the definiteness of the request, and the equal, inevitable, mathematical reaction of something mechanical to that definiteness, delineating that and not something else—because while the Universe is a unity, as Emerson said, the center is unity but the circumference is multiplicity or variation. All things come from the one thing. Philosophy has taught academically—which even psychosomatic medicine does not understand, but comes nearer to it than most forms of medicine—body-mind relations which science doesn't know, medicine doesn't know; only metaphysicians know, not that they are better but they happen to have found this out, and the answer is right here, and it follows there is no difference between the thought and the form it takes. Thoughts are literally things; they do not operate upon things; and this is possible if the Universe in which we live is a system of intelligence, a spiritual system governed by laws which are Intelligence operating mechanically as Law, always producing an inevitable result —two and two will always make four.

Some people were yakking yesterday about something, and I asked them how many people it took to convince them the world is flat. If we were depending on our thought, our willpower, our creativity, our manipulation . . . Jesus said, "Who by taking thought can add one cubit to his stature?" And yet Jesus above all is the one who turns right around and says, "Take thought." But why? "Because it is done unto you." That is the key to "Take thought" and to "Who by taking thought . . . ?" It is a paradox until we understand the subtlety of it.

"It will be done unto you." And this we must accept as the nature of the Universe in which we live. You can't explain it. Don't waste time in trying to explain it. There is more that cannot be explained than can be. Even God could not tell you what God is, because God would have to tell you what God is by comparison with what God is not. Therefore his language is "Yea" and "Amen."

It is absolutely impossible for the Ultimate to know that It is the Ultimate; it is equally impossible for It not to know—and there is a difference. We have to suppose such an absolute as Consciousness and such a reaction as Law and Order; therefore when we give a treatment, as Quimby said (he is the first one who discovered how to give a spiritual mind treatment, and everyone has followed this), the difference is in the similarity only. He said, "I stand as a lawyer stands to his client. Here is a man of opinions but there is a man of wisdom. I explain away the opinions, and you ask me what is my cure, and my answer is, my cure is my explanation." Jesus said, "You will know the truth and the truth will set you free." Quimby was proceeding on the assumption that mind is matter in solution, matter is mind in form; but he said they are both united. Put together, they constitute "the matter of a superior wisdom"—and that is very interesting.

This is completely necessary to understand because

while we say that all is infinite Mind in manifestation, etc., we are supposing something that observes the similarity and interaction and polarization, because there is nothing in the whole universe but polarity between action and reaction. We have to suppose, then, that the reaction is equal and identical with the action, because it is the Omega of its own Alpha, and the one is in the other. The Old Testament says that this is the time when God "made every plant of the field before it was in the earth."

And this makes the treatment dependent upon nothing but clear thinking, logical arguments; or straight affirmations; or unexplained or unspoken realization. These are the only ways we know: Clear thinking, by affirmation and denial, as Kimball* said: This argument, logically presented to mind, produces this result; or prayer of affirmation accepted; or complete realization without argument or prayer or anything else. They will all three work. I think we tend to combine the first and the last—more or less an analysis coupled with a realization. That is about where most of us are.

But always it will be that which supplants one thought with another; and because the whole thing is in an eternal state of liquidity, that which denies the solid will affirm the liquid, and that which denies the liquid will affirm the solid; and the action and reaction will go on this way. So we fall right back upon our own state of consciousness when we give a treatment: how many people will it take to convince us the world is flat? There are not enough in the world.

*Edward A. Kimball, celebrated teacher of Christian Science.

But let us tell ourselves forty times that we have a bad stomach, and the stomach—which is indeterminate, hasn't any sense—would react that way. If we thought harmony enough, it would heal it. Someone says it is all nonsense. Who knows? Never let anybody kid you into thinking you don't know. Never listen to arguments that say the whole world has believed such-and-such. Always somebody has to break the sound barrier, stretch the horizon out further. This is eternal progress. We are betwixt and between that which seems so real and is as real as it is supposed to be, but which has no innate reality, no innate determination, no choice, no mind—like time, the timeless, and eternity. But they all depend on the Old Man.

We don't wave any wands. The only one we wave is compliance with the laws of nature, which work mathematically, the use of which may be inspirational and illuminative, but the reaction to which Jesus was so certain of that he said, "Heaven and earth will pass away, but my words shall not until they are fulfilled."

CHAPTER 12

What Happens When We Give a Treatment

I WANTED TO DISCUSS what happens when we give a treatment. There was a discussion the other day as to whether or not we are a Christian denomination, and I said of course we are a Christian denomination, and several said we are not; I said we are a Christian church, and they agreed to that, because we believe in and follow the teachings of Jesus, the greatest of all Jewish prophets. There were no Christians when Jesus was around; Jesus never heard of a Christian, and he would be amazed if he could come here today and see what we have done to what he said.

It was very interesting to me. As far as the world is concerned, we are a Christian denomination and we wish to be; but Mark* explained to me that we are Christian insofar as we follow the teachings of the Bible and of Jesus, but we are not Christian theologians, because we do not accept what has been attached to it by theology—much of it—and that is rational, I think. We don't believe

*Mark T. Carpenter, Religious Science minister and associate of Ernest Holmes.

184

in devils, in hell, in purgatory or limbo; we don't believe God chose some people to reveal something to, and didn't to others, because that is ridiculous. We believe in *divine patterns*, and not *divine plans*. But all of this Jesus taught together with all other great teachers.

I have been waiting for some years for something like this to come up in our movement, merely to clarify it—because I have never once imposed a personal opinion on our church movement. Whatever I believe I do not try to impose on our ministers or say, "This is what 'we' believe." In my mind we do not believe anything unless we all agree that there are certain things we do agree on. I wouldn't want to be any part of starting another closed system. But having this question come up through a ministers' meeting, now I can tell them what I believe, and they probably will say they believe it; and then we will arrive at what we believe without my imposing what I believe on what they believe, and no one will know the difference. And this is the way to get your own way, if you just have patience.

I was thinking for about two hours after dinner—thinking about treatment; because I don't believe our movement is worth a dime unless *something happens*. We are not just another group of people, nor just another religion, nor just another philosophy or science. In line with Divine Science, Christian Science, and all the other metaphysical movements, we believe in something that is added to the philosophy and the theology of what all the churches believe in. We do not disbelieve what they believe in, fundamentally. In essence they all believe about the same thing. But we do believe this: that we are

185

living in a spiritual Universe right now. The Universe is a spiritual system; it is intelligent and governed by Intelligence. Because it is intelligent, it is a unity. Because there is nothing unlike it with which to divide it, therefore it remains a unity.

That which is a unity—whether we think of a unity small or large—because it is indivisible, it is present in its entirety at any and every point. That is what is meant by the Omnipresence of God. It really is an axiomatic and mathematical and logical proposition that whatever the original Creative Genius is, whatever God is, God is what we are—and there is no difference between the word of Truth we speak and the word of Truth God speaks, because when we speak a word of Truth, it is Truth announcing itself, and that is God. "Who hath seen me hath seen the Father." Emerson said, "Who in his integrity worships God becomes God." It cannot be otherwise.

But since God is infinite, as Troward said, It goes on ad infinitum, but with never any point of saturation, like the sequence of numbers: you never exhaust the possibility of multiplying them by themselves or adding another unit equal to the sum total of the first one.

What we have to arrive at is the significance, first of all, of the intellect—unless we have that far-reaching consciousness of fate and conviction which certainly is wonderful, but which very few people have; and the average person cannot wait, necessarily, for that transition of thought through some inward experience which lifts him, as it were, above the mundane clod to the Seventh Heaven of bliss. He has to start right where he is to go where he is going; and unless by some inward awareness or intuition we grasp the significance of spiritual things, we have to begin by some proposition that will at least acquaint the intellect with the validity of the proposition —Is it so, or is it not so? *Life is*—that is self-evident. Whatever Life is, it is. We choose to call Life by the name of God or Truth or Reality or the Supreme Intelligence or Divine Spirit or Creative Genius or Universal Mind. It doesn't matter what we call it; all these mean the same thing. Life is, or the Truth is that which is. That is the first axiom of reason or self-evident reality.

Now it is self-evident that there can only be one Life, because if there were two and they were opposed to each other, they would neutralize each other. If there appeared to be two and they were just alike, they would coalesce; they wouldn't be two at all. That is why it says, "Hear, O Israel, Eternal the Lord thy God is one." That is why the Hindu said, "What we call matter is Atman, because there is nothing but God." Now they did not use the stupid approach that many modern metaphysicians have taken in order to arrive at the Reality: to deny everything they don't like. This is not the right way. I find that eventually they affirm everything they want to be so and deny everything they don't want to be so. Truth has nothing to do with our human opinion. I would suspect my opinion as much as I would anyone else's.

Truth is what is and not what we think. We may believe what is not so; we can only know what is so.

There is One Life, that Life is God, that Life is my life. Emerson said there is one mind common to all men, etc. They have all announced it. God is one, and there is only one of whatever It is, and this is self-evident. Well, if the One is all there is and It isn't divided, then while our imagination may not include the scope of the reference, our intellect and sense of reality can accept the fact that all of what is (now this is difficult to understand and I don't pretend to understand it, but I accept the fact; it is hard for me to understand that all of the only God there is is between my two fingers here; sounds egotistical and conceited, and it has nothing to do with either) all of the God there is is at any and every point of infinity. That is why Mrs. Eddy said It is neither beyond the point nor approaching it; It is *at* the point—and she is right. And it is why the ancients said It is that whose center is everywhere and whose circumference is nowhere.

I was thinking about these things last night. They are not new to me or to you; but I was thinking about the relationship of this to a treatment, because I had given several treatments, and I thought that one of these treatments didn't sound quite real to me—like you were talking to a void and nothing happened. It seemed like the words went into a vacuum, and it wasn't real to me; what I had said didn't sound real. Treatment is the heart of our work, and without it what have we to offer? Nothing to offer except the proof. We have something to prove, and that is the availability of Presence, of Law, of Person, and of Power—personalizing without ever being personal in the sense of a possession, because at the moment it becomes personal in the sense of a possession, everything we think we possess personally will ultimately obsess us. It is true. I don't care what it is. I am speaking of the essence of things.

This is no different from the Bible saying that we are servants to the thing we obey. Now there is nothing wrong with possession as *use*. It is rather that there can be no such thing as individual good in the Universe: where would it come from, this good that belongs to *me*—? I do not see where there can be an individual anything in the Universe; because if there were, then that individual something, whether blade of grass or archangel, would block the entrance of more universality into itself and could itself never evolve into more universality. The door would be closed. It is logically, mathematically, and intuitively certain that this is so. That is why Emerson said, "Cast your good on the four winds of heaven," and Whitman said, "The gift is most to the giver and comes back to him"; and Jesus said, "Give and it shall be given unto you," etc.

Now to get back to the other proposition: it is not by merit of any virtue we possess that truth is truth; we are only fortunate if we see it and understand it and accept it. And I was thinking I had given two or three treatments that sounded pretty real to me; and when I think one and it doesn't sound real, I start all over again and say it out loud. Did you ever try that? Sometimes it does something, because sometimes the thought seems nebulous. We have to treat, in situations like this, that only the truth can be known, only the truth can be revealed, and only the truth can be accepted, and only the truth can be acted upon. That will cover any case at law or any place else. We can work to know there is nothing but the truth; no one can utter anything but the truth; no one can believe anything but the truth or listen to anything but the truth or act upon anything but the truth. This we have a right to do, and it has nothing to do with our opinion. Then I said to myself, "What power is back of the word

I am speaking?" Would you think anyone who has been in this sort of work as long as I have would have to get right back to "c-a-t spells cat," etc.—?

It surprises me; but believe me, I don't hesitate to do it, because I know if we jump a hoop here and run around and nothing happens, there is something fundamentally wrong—and we can all get confused and make mistakes. So I said, "Get right back here. What is back of my word?" And then I said, "There is nothing back of my word. If I have a word that is ineffective, there can't be anything back of it. Nothing of conviction is going into it, and I have been merely announcing what I hoped might happen tomorrow."

Hazel* used to say to me, "Be sure your treatment is not just your desire or wistful wishing; be certain that when you are through with it, the Law and Order of the Universe is behind it and you have nothing to do with it. It is none of your business." The treatment is no good until it is that way: it is the authority of Truth and not of the one who announces it. The moment it becomes the authority of the one who announces it, he is holding a thought, sending out a thought, willing something, concentrating.

At a meeting recently someone was to give a treatment, and they had so many things to do before they could give the treatment that I couldn't treat at all, and I got confused. We have something that the world is waiting for, the proof that the most simple person can do. He doesn't have to be able to read Greek or Latin; he doesn't have

---

*Hazel Holmes, Ernest Holmes' wife and a skillful practitioner.

to arrive at the exalted place where we only see a shadow. This is it: "The words I speak, they are Spirit and they are Life." So I said, "What goes on?" And then I said, "I think probably I am sending thoughts out, and that isn't what I want to do. I am trying to make something happen, and that is not the way the Universe is organized. It cannot be." Then I thought, "It can only happen inside of me anyway—my treatment is my acceptance." The word itself, I think, is a mold. I don't think the word is a creative thing. It appears to be one; but let's say it isn't exactly that.

Jesus did not teach superstitions, he did not teach or say the things that theology said he said or taught. He said things that they interpreted to mean what he didn't. He said, "I am the way, the truth, and the life. No man cometh unto the father but by me." He is talking about Atman, Christ, Buddha, Truth, the Spiritual Man. The only mediator between God and man is Christ. This has nothing to do with Jesus. Jesus was the greatest of the Jewish prophets, a Jewish boy; Christ is the same as Buddha, the Enlightened One, the Perfect Man—the perfected man. And so I finally said, "It is none of my business, I neither know nor care anything about what happens. But this I know: nothing can be misrepresented; only the truth will be known. There isn't anything or anyone who can articulate a falsehood, or anyone to believe one; nothing to act on what isn't so—because what isn't so isn't so, and that is that." This morning the word came through that it was so.

I could not complete this treatment while I was trying to get it outside myself. This is what I discovered, and this is why I am interested in it. While I tried to make this treatment do anything or be anywhere other than where it was, it got separated from me and I didn't know whether it went anywhere or not. It is a funny, illusive thing, but a real one. And I thought, "I have taught this so long that maybe I have forgotten what it means"—and this too can be true. We can be so darned theoretical it doesn't work. And I thought again: in the present state of our existence, every layman must be a practitioner; it is no good if he isn't. I just want everyone to know there is such a thing as a treatment, there is such a thing as a Principle that reacts. They do know how to do it; what they know is the way to do it. But they may not be sure they know— and the way they know is the way it works. This is the illusive thing.

Everyone believes all things are possible to God. Almost everyone today believes theoretically in what you and I believe; most of them do—you almost never find anyone who doesn't. They may interpret it differently and have a superstition or ignorance about it, but most people believe there is Something that can do anything. But how few people, even in our own field, know! But the word, in my estimation, is not the essence or mold—a word without a meaning, without an acceptance in the mind of the one who utters it.

Then I started reading Aurobindo again, and it starts out by saying that we will never get anywhere while we believe in a spiritual Universe operating on a material one or a physical one, which is so true. Einstein said that energy and mass are one, and Quimby said that mind is matter in solution and matter is mind in form, but there is a superior Intelligence to which they or it are as "the matter of Spirit"—which is same thing. All these people have reduced the Universe to a fluidic Something, taking a temporary form.

Did you ever read Eustace's* book on Christian Science simplified? I don't care where it comes from, it is a good book, and Truth is always Truth and doesn't belong to anyone. In this he said, we don't spiritualize matter or materialize Spirit; we are not using a spiritual power to operate on a physical one, else we shall be using some power to operate upon the inertia of a resistance. And as long as we operate upon the inertia of a resistance, we shall be resisting it—and we shall rise little higher than the contention of a struggle where opposites that are more or less equal contend or crash, like two icebergs, rather than getting some other thing up there which melts them. We are not trying to get a Spiritual Universe to operate on a physical one. We are not trying to get a word of Truth to operate on a word of untruth. This too is dualism. We are not trying to get a good to overcome an evil. There is no evil in the Universe—you know what I mean—and if there is, where did it come from? But there is certainly a mistaken concept of what is good; the illusion is not even in the simplest fact but in our reaction to it. The earth and the sky do not meet out there—but there *is* an earth and a sky. I don't feel we have to even deny experience; you certainly do not have to deny fact to affirm a faith, because, as I read, the larger order includes everything. The greater includes the lesser.

We have to get away not only from contemplation of

*Herbert Eustace, teacher of Christian Science and author of *Christian Science: Its Clear, Correct Teaching.*

dualism in our system but even so far as possible from the further mental contention of explaining to ourselves that since there is no dualism, our word is going to work; because in this is a subtle negation—and even in this affirmation—because the mind may only affirm, even though it does it negatively. There is no dualism in the Universe; on this we agree. There appears to be, and on this we are agreed too. We have to get to a place where appearance is not something to be contested against or fought, but merely be clarified by knowing it isn't.

The subtleness of the mind is the most illusive thing in the world, and in this very illusiveness is the key to success or failure. Someone I think quite a little of is away, distant; here is what looks like quite a proposition and has to be neutralized; and adding this all up together, I have created an adversary. And once you have an adversary, you have to fight with him or he will cut your throat. And this is subtle. Here is this very innocent illusiveness, probably the key to success or failure.

Troward talked about the way to know whether we are treating in the Absolute. But I don't like that expression, because it looks as though you had to go from the relative to the Absolute, which you don't—and which he didn't mean. But too many absolutists interpret it that way. Relativity is as absolute as Absoluteness, because it is Absoluteness at the point of Its own relativity, that it may express Itself; and there is no dualism in it. That is true. Plotinus said that everything is as real as it is supposed to be, but nothing has self-determination. It is quite a thing to dare, sometimes, to come honest with yourself —but how revealing it is! And that is the trouble; and we hate to look at it.

And yet until I am willing to, then I am the guy who has to live with myself all the time. So I thought, "Start all over again. None of this is any of your business. You have dragged in more things to get rid of, and while you have them, there they are." So finally I was able to get to the place where I could say, "Truth is all there is; there is nothing else. Nothing can happen but what is so; nothing can be believed in except what is so; nothing else can be acted upon; no one can articulate or act on something that isn't so, because there is no one else to speak."

So by the time I got through, I felt about 50 to 75 pounds lighter physically—because a mental burden is a physical one. There is a book which starts out by saying, "We used to think a person has to be well in order to be happy. We now know a person has to be happy in order to be well—and this is not putting the cart before the horse."

Then I thought about something else: all this wouldn't be so much to me if I didn't keep on thinking, "Why is it so?" But we cannot explain life. God couldn't tell you why God is God. There is no God who can do anything other than announce. And this is why it is that the more exalted the mysticism in the teachings of the world, the less the explanation. Jesus never explained anything; he said it is like this and like that and like something else. The greater they have been, the less they have explained and the more they have announced.

However I feel this: very few people have this mysticism, and very few people understand what they are talking about. We go through processes of reasoning to arrive at that which could not reason; but if it did, it would be reasonable. Jesus said, "I judge no man; but if I did, my judgment would be just." All of our processes of reasoning are merely methods whereby we arrive at that which knows no process and operates by announcement, involved within which announcement are the processes of the evolution of the idea which the word has involuted.

This is what Troward explains in the first chapter of *Bible Mystery, Bible Meaning*—the chapter on Involution and Evolution—and what the Bible explains in the beginning of Genesis where it says this is the generation of time when God "made every plant of the field before it was in the earth"—and it means what Browning meant when he said, "A spark disturbs our clod" and what Whitman meant when he said, "At the center of everything nestles the seed of perfection," etc. All evolution—we do not deny evolution, you know—is the logical unfoldment of involution.

Ouspensky* said that we go down a street and see a house, but traveling in this direction we only see a small part of it; someone coming from the other direction sees another part of the house. Now nothing happens to the house. If we were in a position where we could see all four sides, we would see them all at once. The other three sides were not absent merely because we couldn't see them. And Aurobindo explained the same thing where he said that whatever is going to evolute throughout eternity had to be involuted, and that all processes of evolution are merely the unfoldment of what is involuted. This is all a grand idea of a universal thing which they have all taught: involution and evolution—that in the original

---

*P. D. Ouspensky, Russian philosopher and writer on asbstract mathematical theory.

meaning, it is the divine spark impregnating the mundane clod, or Lucifer thrown over the embankments of heaven, falling to the earth like a flaming sword. It all means the Light that lighteth every man's path. It means the Light of Life impregnating this, and now It is this clod—matter is Brahma; manifestation is God. Mrs. Eddy said the same thing when she said, "All is Mind and its infinite manifestation," because their whole process of treatment is based on the assumption that there is no difference between the thought and the thing—and I think that is correct.

This will hold true, then, in our treatment: that the nature of Reality is such that God didn't will it—there are no cosmic plans; God isn't going somewhere. Dean Inge said that an infinite will is a contradiction of both logic and mathematics, and that is true. So the whole creative process of evolution or unfoldment is merely an effect, and it is of the nature of Reality. Therefore this is the reason why if I treat I don't convince anything but myself: there is only one Self, and It really doesn't have to be convinced. But I have to break through my intellect to the place where my whole being emotionally and intellectually may *accept*, and not even look for the evidence; because to it the word will be the evidence. "The words I speak, they are Spirit and Life."

So let's let it happen here—and know that our word is the presence and power and activity of the Living Spirit. We don't make it; it can't help it; we have nothing to do with it or to say about it—it is transcendent. We don't will it, wish it; it is so. And we know "There is that which scattereth and increaseth"; there is that gathered which is scattered; and all the power and presence there is is Light and Love, the Living Spirit Almighty—and I shall forever be. That which I am is now; what God is is now what I am. "I am that which Thou art, and Thou art that which I am," the eternal song, the living joy, stillness of peace, security of love, joy of action. I am That; and in this which I am is all life, all motion, all action, reaction, every song, every dance and wind and waves and splendor of the sunset and song of bird—and love of children, and mother pregnant with hope and father joyous in the giving and ineffable beauty, over all, in all, and through all. So it is.

CHAPTER 13

Prayer Must Be Affirmative

THERE IS SO MUCH that we seem to have forgotten about what we used to know about the simplicity of this thing. Did you read the article in the *Times* this morning about the Episcopal clergyman and what he had to say about prayer? That shows a tendency of the times. It is a metaphysical article; it said that prayer must be affirmative. Now from our viewpoint we get right back to what Quimby said—and everyone said that he was an infidel and charlatan; remember, this was 100 years ago, and he was the first who ever discovered that there is such a thing as what we call affirmative prayer, and how it works, in the whole history of the world that we have any record of—he said that Jesus did his work *with understanding*; that if he were healing with faith, he would have been a humbug. Mrs. Eddy said somewhere that if we are healing *by* faith, we ought to get healed *of* faith so we can heal with understanding—not in those exact words.

I told you some time ago I knew a Methodist bishop 45 years ago who said the time would come when all Christian Science pagodas would be upside down in hell. Here is a radical departure from the concept of prayer when we consider that down here at Redlands University they discovered that the affirmative prayer, which Cherry* Parker called Prayer Therapy, is 70 percent more effective than the ordinary prayer right straight through the line, so that too arrives at a principle. The thing that Quimby and Mrs. Eddy and early New Thought teachers believed, and all of the metaphysical field that differs from the other concept of prayer, is right here. And when we inquire into it, then, and when we analyze it to see what it really means—not just on the surface—we have to accept that the prayer is its own answer in the terms of its own acceptance. We can't avoid it. Don't you think that is right? *The prayer is its own answer in the terms of its own acceptance.*

Jesus said, "It is done unto you as you believe"; therefore we have to accept that nothing can come out of the prayer unless it is put into the prayer. And yet no power is put into it. It is taken out. It is something of a paradox; but we don't put power into life—we take it out always. We don't put anything into anything. As Emerson said, "We are beneficiaries of the divine fact." Browning, putting it poetically, said, "It is Thou, God, who giveth; it is I who receive." And Jesus went around telling everybody to believe and have faith—it is done unto you as you believe—and then turns right around and says, "But who by taking thought can add one cubit to his stature?" We have to reconcile all these apparent opposites to find the kernel inside the nut that is really edible.

*Nickname of William Parker. See William R. Parker and Elaine St. Johns, *Prayer Can Change Your Life* (Prentice-Hall, 1957).

This is very important, because if we are going to teach a science of religion or Christianity; or applied, or practical, Christianity; if we are going to accentuate even what Parker discovered down here—to put it down in a form that all superstition is removed from; if we are going to do all this, then we are going almost to be shocked ourselves, and a little mystified, because life is a mysterious thing. I gave the best talk on prayer Sunday night; wish I had had it taken down. Nothing new—but it came together so well. It came up that if we compare the concept of Jesus as absolute intuition—and he said, "It is done unto you as you believe"—and the way we think of it as a scientific thing, in that we know what goes and how and what to expect, then we are going to have to arrive at the conclusion that nothing comes out of the prayer. Now this is the treatment, other than what we put into it; and yet what we put into it is now the power that makes it what it is. And yet it must be we who put it in.

If we didn't, one kind of prayer wouldn't be any better than another. Some very good things happened last Tuesday here, and they can't happen unless the treatment is its own answer and unless there is no difference between the treatment and what it does. And that is why it is we never try to repeat a treatment and give it twice alike. There are no formulas for treatment. Our daily meditations are not formulas; they are merely inspirational readings for the purpose of getting someone into an attitude. You will find that all Christian Science practitioners read *Science and Health* all the time. They do not read it as a formula, but to keep their mind as, we will say, in tune. It is probably a good idea. When you get so you don't have to read any meditation, you will have one more savior out of your way—you will be that much nearer the thing you are after, because, as Emerson said, "We are that much weaker for that one who marches under our banner." Isn't that interesting? These are only instrumentalities, like an automobile or something we ride is; they are not the destination. That is why Emerson said that travel is a fool's paradise.

But to get back to the essence of the thing: if a prayer is 70 percent more effective if it is an affirmation, that is the right way to pray. We are sure of that. If some affirmative prayers are much better than others—which our experience teaches us; we are sure about that—if there is no formula about a prayer which we know is true, then every prayer or treatment is a spontaneous thing or proclamation of the mind knowing it. And if all that is true, then we know that the answer to the prayer is in the prayer when it is prayed. This is what is shocking—and yet we don't put it in; we take it out. We know it as well as we know that the chicken is in the egg when you set the hen, and that the oak tree is in the acorn when you plant the acorn. But if these things are so, then we find, again, the place of what we call realization as an acceptance; but we find something else that I was never quite so clear about as I was Sunday night. Isn't that funny!

So this is a new sidelight in my own mind on the scientific angle. There were a number of university students there who belong to University of Colorado, and this guy tells me that they set up a terrible argument with him, and question everything—but they come. So I made a few answers, and one of the boys, who is an honor student, came up afterwards and said, "Would you speak at the

University? I could get a very large group there." And I asked if it would be a waste of time or if they were really interested, and he said they were really interested. I finally got this insight and said, "We may view it poetically; we may view it inspirationally; we may view it intuitively; but according to experiments down at Redlands, they didn't view it any of these ways. This is what is important about it—that it did not come out of another religion; because if it had, it would have lost much of its value. It is up to us to find out what the rightness is. They took from every stratum—doctors, students, lawyers, whoever would come—and these people didn't have any great religious conviction; they just said, 'Let us experiment.'"

Quimby said that if Jesus had healed by faith, he would have been a charlatan, and that is shocking; and Mrs. Eddy said that you have to get healed of your faith before you can heal with understanding—and she was right too. And yet there is nothing wrong with faith. Faith does also comply with the condition, and would comply without understanding. But you cannot teach faith. You cannot teach consciousness. Through contact with someone who has consciousness we may gain it. That is why people read certain people, why they will go to hear certain people. Anyone who has a consciousness will impart it to the audience. Jesus said, "If these people didn't cry out, the rocks would have to." He knew that they ought to be absolutely still without noise; but terrific, titanic impact was being made between himself and people around him in the ethers of the universe, and he said, "It is no wonder they are screaming. If they didn't, the rocks would have to jump up and holler because something is happening."

Now Jesus was not a mere sentimentalist. He never departed from logic. He was as profound as Plato or Socrates—but so simple that nobody believed it; and they don't now. And you will find if you read the teachings of Jesus very carefully that he had just two things to teach: a divine Presence and a universal Law—nothing else. Everything else comes under this—all the beauty, everything; a penetrating vision to see the one, and an acceptance to do the other. "Blessed are the pure in heart, for they shall see God." Only the pure in heart can see God because Love only knows and comprehends Love. Beauty only understands Beauty. Peace knows nothing about discord. Tranquility knows nothing about confusion. Faith knows nothing about fear. Heaven knows nothing about hell. But we get right back to the basis upon which our whole practical application is organized or made. These people down here at the University didn't have any particular faith; they were a group of people who merely did what somebody told them to do. You know, it is the most difficult thing in the world to make an ordinary person understand what a treatment is—to cause him to see how simple it is, then to get him to know *This is it,* and he knows what it is, and he knows how to use it; then to get him to use it in that simple way, and then get him to accept that what he has done is right and he may expect a result. It is the most difficult thing in world.

People will listen endlessly and endlessly to abstractions they don't understand at all and not get anywhere; and Jesus knew this and said it is like a child. But he never overlooked the profundity. He taught a divine Presence with which or whom we may commune, and that our word is the presence and power and activity of a creative cause which creates the situations it would experience out of its own know-how and its own "know-be." And its own "be" is something which nothing, neither God nor man, can explain—because if you were to personalize God and say, "Now God, how did you get to be God?" He wouldn't know what you were talking about. In other words, the Ultimate cannot explain the Inexplicable; the Ultimate *is* the Inexplicable. That is why the first axiom of rationality says that the truth is what is, and we have to assume that there is "what is," or nothing would be.

"I am that which I am, beside which there is none other"—and we have to get 150 people to believe that they know what a spiritual mind treatment is, to understand what it is, to accept *this is it*, to agree that they are good enough, know enough, and have learned enough to do it and say, "This is it," and then get them to do it. There would be a dynamic something created that never happened before—and this is what I am interested in. It seems to me that everyone in our field should be interested in this. It is so inspiring that I don't know how anyone can help being enthusiastic about it. This is the most creative act that is known to the mind of man—treatment. It is the most creative thing the mind of man can engage in—because without tools, brushes, or pigments or forms or instruments, something happens creatively, merely as a result of something you think inside yourself. You don't even do it—because "Who by taking thought can add one cubit to his stature?" But you think it, because it is done unto those who believe. And the very fact that it is done unto those who believe is added to the thought that you cannot add one cubit to your stature by thinking, and put together by the thought that belief, which is thought, does it—and we shall find again, to get back to the pinpoint of the complete abstraction, that the reason for it all is that we are dealing with Self-Existence. That is the secret, the key. But Self-Existence is not easy for us to imagine, merely because it isn't easy for us to accept the very simple fact that the whole nature of the Universe is Self-Existence, that there has to be That which makes things out of Itself by Itself becoming what It makes through the law of Its own Being, which will have to be absolute—and that God didn't make It; It *is* God. It is part of the dual nature of the Infinite. Not dual as duality but, let us say, as attributes—the beingness of the Being.

But these things that we have to accept are difficult merely because we haven't made them easy; because the scientist, strangely enough, accepts in his field what people in our field will have to learn to accept, which is the great simplicity of no longer arguing as to why or even what the principle is that they accept, because they have demonstrated that it exists.

We have to do the same thing. It is what they all do: they don't say what is energy? what is life? what is thought? what is the mind? what is the soul? Only theologians tear themselves apart over these silly questions. Emerson said everything, and they said he was an infidel. But he was smart; and people still don't know it. *It is the complete acceptance*—and it is the most difficult thing in the world about treatment. But there is nothing can deny it, nothing can stop it, nothing to say it can't be or hadn't ought to be, nothing to limit it, nothing that has to help it or boost it or support it. It is what it is because of the self-existence of the creative consciousness of the Infinite, which is the only consciousness that there is—which is our consciousness in such degree as we are aware of it. That is the way it works. Is that clear? But it is so darned simple—who among us is going to accept it?

I can say to 150 people, "You are going to come here every Sunday morning, and do this thing (not these words) every day for 10 or 15 minutes, according to the occasion." This is a project, and they actually do it. I wouldn't be surprised if some Sunday morning the roof would take off and float out over the ocean—and as Jesus said, if the people didn't scream, the rocks would have to. This is conviction. This is the thing Jesus had. He didn't say anything that was new to the world. The stuff they discovered recently and say the Essenes had said— God is in the rock and plant—Hindus had said: "Lift the rock and you will find Me, cleave the wood for there am I." All the beatitudes have been said a thousand times. The difference between Jesus and some of them was that Jesus knew what the words meant. Anybody can say to a paralyzed man, "Stretch forth your hand." But who would *expect* it to stretch forth?

There couldn't have been any difference in the mind of this man—at least it seems to me that there would have been no difference—between his saying, "Get up and walk," and the guy getting up and walking. I don't believe there was any difference. I think this is just as Einstein said—energy and mass are equal; Einstein said this same thing scientifically, did you know this? He didn't say one operates upon the other; he didn't say one influences the other. And we do not say that we spiritualize matter or materialize spirit. We say one *is* the other; they are the same. Ice is water, and water is ice; but not all water is ice, and ice is not all the water there is. There is a lot more of it. Jesus said, "Not I, but the Father who dwelleth in me; but the Father who dwelleth in me is greater than I; and yet it is This who dwelleth in me that is what I am. Whatsoever the Son seeth the Father do, that doth the son also, that the Father may be glorified in the Son," etc.

You will notice in his healing, which you and I will call his demonstration, Jesus was not beseeching or praying. Jesus communed, recognized, unified, and worked by *command*, but not by an arbitrary command—to scream an affirmation at an empty void or into a vacuum of endless space. But you know, right now as I talk about it, I could just get up and scream like hell—it is the way I feel about it. There was a guy who came Sunday, and he said, "Do you talk in Los Angeles?" and I said no. He said, "If you are ever going to give a talk, let us know and we will fly out to hear it." I thought, this guy doesn't have to fly anywhere. He has already been where he is going. He doesn't want to hear me; something happened to him, so he listened to himself, perhaps. All revelation is self-revelation. All healing is self-healing. All truth is self-truth. All the God we pray to, and the only God we *could* pray to, is the effort of the mind to discover itself, being the thing it is in search after. This is the center from which Jesus talked. It isn't conceit, because you have nothing to do with it. That is why the Gita says that the self must raise the self by self.

Now if we got the thing cornered and captured and caught where we know what it is and where it is, how stupid we are that we don't do better with it! But we get right back to that simple thing. We are not stupid; as simple as this thing is, it is the most revolutionary thought that ever came to the world—now not what I am saying

—but what Jesus said, and what they all said, and what we reiterated. It is the most revolutionary thought that ever came to the world. That is why Emerson said, "Beware when God lets loose a thinker on this planet." Governments, institutions, political systems, economic systems —everything is going to change, because there is something shattering about this thing. It will level all. But believe me, when God does let loose a thinker—of course, God doesn't let loose of them; they loose themselves in God—he will speak a language so simple people will not accept it. It has to be that way—the most startling thing, intellectually and philosophically; because 90 percent of psychology as it is taught is materialistic; at least 90 percent of all theology in the world—every kind—is dualistic; and most philosophy is materialistic. It has tended to change in the last 25 years, but it is still over on the side of dualism and materialism and will be until it recognizes the similarity of the visible and invisible—energy and mass—what appears and what doesn't appear—and, in regard to our field, in practical application, until it knows what you and I are talking about. I don't claim to know it; I just know it is true. There couldn't be one bit of difference between what we say and what happens when we say it, because *what we say* is *the thing doing*, announcing itself as *the thing done*, and existing in a medium where time does not exist and space does not enclose—a medium of absolute freedom, of spontaneous combustion or self-announcement. This is the secret Jesus knew.

But he knew it in such a human way. He called one of his followers and named him after the God of thunder and lightning, because this guy got mad one day and wanted Jesus to call down anathemas on somebody who had laughed at them. Jesus was one of the funniest men who ever lived. We don't like to think this way, because we think it's sacrilegious. All these old guys came in and wanted to stone the prostitute, and Jesus had a lot of fun with them. This is real, the essence of a very subtle wit. He said, All right, you have all the answers—and being completely pure and without sin, you take her out and slit her throat. This is high wit in my estimation.

But there was that thing about Jesus—when he said, "Let it be done," there wasn't any stammering or stuttering; he didn't turn pale or shake. This was to Jesus like a child saying, "Pass the bread," knowing it will be passed. That is why he said, "If ye ask bread, will you get a stone?" Jesus knew the exactness of the Law. Jesus knew no one beseeched God. God is the bread. God is the stone too—or else there wouldn't be a stone. As we discussed the other day, the emotions of love and hate are the same energy; but being channeled differently, it becomes an emotion of love or an emotion of hate. But it is an identical energy. The only thing in the world that can make it work is what made it appear not to work; the only thing that can make it appear not to work is what makes it work; else you have dualism in the universe. We have not got a good and bad; we have not got a right and wrong; we have not got an impossible ethics and morals in the universe. We only have action and reaction, the sole nature of which action has to be in harmony and what we call love and givingness, or it would destroy itself; and since it hasn't, it is.

We don't have to argue whether God is love or not, or whether God is givingness. We don't have to argue whether this Thing is good or whether It is joy or beauty or peace—there can be no argument against It. Science knows no energy that will operate against itself. What do we argue with? And we certainly do a lot of arguing, don't we!

Our spiritual conviction is arguing with our psychological self. That is good, and it's worth an hour's talking to say, That is it. Our spiritual conviction is arguing with the psychological reaction, which is largely unconscious. Hazel* used to say that we are so marked by experience. She was the wisest person I ever knew, and she had no superstition. She used to say, "The Universe is just, without judgment." What do people mean when they have to recite the Lord's prayer, or something you or someone else wrote for a treatment? Don't they know that a treatment is an entity in itself—that what will come out of it is what goes into it, nothing more and nothing less—? It cannot be less, and it would be impossible for it to be more—because this is the measure-upper. Take a 2-gallon pail and lift up out of infinity 2 gallons of liquid: you will have just 2 gallons in the pail. That is all the pail holds.

Our psychological self contains the memory of the whole human race. I thoroughly agree with Jung's concept of the collective unconscious; it is no different than Mrs. Eddy's idea of mortal mind, and the Bible's of the carnal mind; but to make it more simple: just what everybody has always believed impinges upon all of us. We don't even know why we are Democrats or Republicans —it is mostly because we are Northerners or Southerners. We have no real rational, intelligent reason at all, do we.

There are logical reasons, yes; but if we had been born

*Hazel Holmes, Ernest Holmes' wife (d. 1957).

211

Baptists, we would be Baptists, etc. At any rate, we shouldn't compare it to our theology, because they are mostly nonsense anyway, but we should compare it to our belief and reaction to life itself. How many people in the world believe they could say to a paralyzed man, "Get up and walk" and have him do it? One man did it. Why don't people believe they can do these things? Practically everybody in the word believes there is *some* power that could do all the things Jesus did. But how many would attach themselves to that power, or it to them? Right in our own field: how many people in this room believe he or she is the one who could do it?

We are getting down to cases, and this is what we have to accept; and we cannot accept it while we believe we *have* to do it. We cannot accept it until we know we *can* do it. And here is the paradox; and this is why Jesus said, "It is done unto you as you believe;" "but who by taking thought can add a cubit to his stature?" This is what Quimby and Mrs. Eddy and the whole field have contended, and what the theological field has never known or seen or understood—and it is interesting to see the first glimmering of this faint flickering of the eyelashes looking up and saying . . . Jesus said, "Behold!" And they all looked up and said, "We don't see a thing!" But Jesus saw something; and what he saw was real and dynamic.

We can *say* that the cancer doesn't have to be there, the tumor doesn't have to be there, the poverty doesn't have to be there, the itch doesn't have to be there; but then we get into a quandary about ourselves, and our teachers say, "Look at me and die—you are not good enough yet." And all this is silly. We don't get right down and say, "Here is a guy who took them right off the campus and said, 'I am not worried and don't care about your theology; just try praying, and *believe* in your own prayer—and let's see what happens.'" A group of untrained people, raw recruits. So why don't we forever put all superstition out? Why don't we forever brush aside, and not say, we are not good enough—? Who told us we were not good enough?—What is good? A very relative term.

We put off the day; we deny that which we will have to affirm. And I will admit every claim about not being good enough, etc.—but I will still say, jump in the water and see if you won't get wet. And anyone who will pray affirmatively will get a result. But we will carry it further and say it cannot be that way unless the thought is the thing, and unless one is merely the liquid form and the other just exactly as Quimby said: mind is matter in solution, matter is mind in form; but there is a superior wisdom which uses them both. If we want to think, and not accept things on another or higher altitude of faith—which is good—then somewhere along the line faith must pass into knowledge, and knowledge into understanding, and understanding into acceptance, and acceptance into announcement. That is the way it was with Jesus. He didn't try to explain very much; he just announced it.

We have to get to a place where we say, *This is it*. Then something comes up—inertia, thought patterns, argument of error, psychic unconscious. A few idealists said there could be peace on earth. Others said, "What fools! There has always been war and always will be war." Russia doesn't want war, and certainly no other country wants war. No one wants war. But it is a psychological thing, something coming up out of the experience of the human race. And the day the consensus of human opinion would agree that there will be no more war—it just won't be there; the affirmation will have neutralized the negation. In all probability we demonstrate a harmony not too much beyond the consensus of human opinion over hundreds of years. There must be a song beyond what any human being has sung—and there is.

But the argument, inertia, spiritual awareness meeting the psychological experience of the ages meets a very worthy adversary—it is less than something and more than nothing. I read an article several years ago, called "I Saw the King of Hell," about a newspaperman and group over in Tibet somewhere where they meet once a year to demonstrate that they can overcome evil. They concentrate, and this takes the form of a gigantic man—an awful-looking thing; they conjure this thing up so everyone can see it. Then after bringing all this about—it is the personification of evil—they have to dissolve it to prove they can control evil, and they do.

Aren't we always seeing these things? Experience is arguing to us, "You can't do this or that"; and the consensus of human opinion is right there. And because someone will give up the so-called evils, and someone else endlessly prays, treats, concentrates, and something happens, we go into a still more illusive form of superstition (and I hate to say this; Emerson said, "Truth is like a cannonball") and we begin to talk about "dedication," etc.; and I believe in all this; but this isn't what makes it work. You would fall into as great an error here as if you were presenting it in a much more crude form. The guy who is drunk and the guy who is in ecstasy before an altar of his faith are the same guy using the same energy, identified with two purposes but seeking the same end, which is gratification, happiness, wholeness, security, and love. That is all anybody is after. There isn't anybody after anything else, no matter what he thinks. There is nothing else he can be after.

Let's get back, back, beyond our badness, goodness, wrong—way out there where there is nothing but space; way down there before we began to think, so there is no liability; get up where there is no noise, no confusion, no traffic, where nothing was ever done or said by ourselves, through all the ages, that alters the fact one iota: the sun still shines. Each take the name of someone and say, "This is happening; whatever is there that doesn't belong is removed, and what should be there is there." Let's know we exist in this place that time does not contain and space does not enclose. Everything we touch is made whole; the light comes through; everything has joy and responsiveness and love—and we are that thing now.

Benediction

THAT IS THE best thing I have said this morning; it is a guarantee that God doesn't figure relatively, but announces absolutely. Well, let's you and me do that. That is a good place to start.

We know we are That; "I am that which Thou art." There are many requests for healing—and will each of you who made those requests think of them and the person you are working for and let's see if we can't realize that the Undivided Whole is right here, the Perfect right here, the Changeless, the All in all. And knowing that by the immutable Law of Self-Existence that which we announce must appear, the water must turn into wine because the word *wine* is used instead of *water*, what we call the healing must take place because it is merely the reaction to the word we are using. We don't put anything into it. We cannot take out all until we stop trying to put in any. It is impossible. Who put the chicken in the egg or the oak tree in the acorn? Only Life can give life. Therefore these persons whose names we have mentioned must be whole right now. We haven't anything to do with it, and it can't help it; and everything that doesn't belong must leave—it is banished; while "All that is at all/ lasts ever past recall."

So our own consciousness is lifted up to the perception of the allness of that which we are, because it is what we are. Now we know that our own consciousness is aware and alive and awake and conscious and perfect. So it is.

NOT THE END
BUT
THE BEGINNING